# Ranger
## (Volume II)

## Theodore Enslin

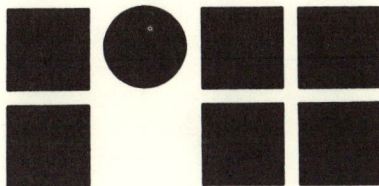

**NORTH ATLANTIC BOOKS**

**Ranger (Volume II)**

ISBN 0-913028-75-4 hardcover (limited signed edition)
ISBN 0-913028-74-6 pbk.

Publisher's Address:

North Atlantic Books
635 Amador Street
Richmond, California 94805

Thanks are due to Station Hill Press, where sections 122 and 128 appeared as a separate booklet, and to Truck Press, sections 129-133 in *Truck* 20.

This project is partially supported by a grant from the National Endowment for the Arts in Washington, D.C., a Federal agency.

This book was set in 10 point Baskerville by Lynn Behrendt at Open Studio in Barrytown, N.Y., a non-profit facility for independent publishers and individual artists, funded in part by grants from the New York State Council on the Arts & the National Endowment for the Arts.

Cover: Lucy Baker

for Mark Hedden

# Book IV

## CXIX

The widespreading sound —
some part of it —
and one part
such bad timing.
(Turning?)
What could have happened?
How should it have been done?
Man, I'd have cleaned ditches
and hoped.
Nothing alive is old —
grows old —
the sea is a young bride —
green manes of hair,
a green youth.
And the land above it,
massed.
Fountains perpetual.
A man in his footsteps
stops short
only as he dies.
His age? Ah, guess it!
Suspended between the earth
and the sea, procrustean,
he remains the only age.
Now wisdom.
The wise must flourish,
and to flourish? in those flowers.
It is young!
Marking time will not do it.
Slow shuffle
is the waltz of death.
(Heaven opens for a moment.
Ah!
        to say the difficult things
without that gravity.
Tilted, and the weight distributed.)
Things of the same time and genus
will grow up together —
crowd, but not destroy.
But if one dies,

and it is replaced,
it is no replacement.
Impoverished, bitter,
that fruit is poison.
The genes scale down.
It ends in hatred —
holding against the last freeze.
Equals:
              hatred.
Get it from cabbages or kings.
Equals:
              the same.
Equals —
              (and I had the cabbages.)
It could — of course it could —
come from other things.
To increase desire
                        lowers
the possibility.
Catch it while it comes —
the sound that overspreads.

We get light *after*
we get dark.

**As I light my lamps
too early**

To put our light
into what is light
kills both.
We die, too, in the process.
Sources,
              but we lose our sources
in the shadows.
The corners of the room turn round.
Nothing has edge
within the afterlight.
Silent, but the silence grows as voice.
The voice of silence,
                        great-throated,
blood-pour over the flood of senses.
Conscious/sentient/
all within the light.
I make my case for it,
and I am held apart.

432

(Sit long enough, the pre-light —
sounds of birds
                    -abraying-
soft purl of the stream.)
 A voice out of the wall:
'Have you lost it?'
'What would it be?'
'The key?'
'Do you go back?'
'Can you move?'
But they were not rules of conduct —
the sound, widespreading,
can't quite repeat itself.
It is not tempered,
or the temper is its own steel —
not melded with any other —
tense/spread.

Leaping out from the center,
what can be found there?
not a dim philosophy,
only the tools,
and the bright ones: used.
Burned shards,
good only to nourish others.
It leads to a dark night,
and a time of playing —
straying
                    over.
FULL UNISON!
DIAPASON,
                    and dispersal.
What sounds is sound itself.
Do not tamper with it.
Despair at utmost —
how? will it go on?
or must it?
(Corpse glitter in the grass —
a drop of mist collected,
and unison in quiet.

So, where very day is like another,
becomes another in its sequence,
none resemble — only in the mind.

And this full darkness blotting out the sun,
relieves, or points up, silence —
area of gall and canker.
Can anything we say go further
than nostalgia? Is there a word?
set of them?
                    I remember — —
All of it flattens out — remembering.
There is spirit in old wood
that mocks us.
                    Bravery falls flat —
is mere bravado.
There is a great deal I'd do,
and do not do:
Wondering, and idly touching keys
-not for the music-
but to bring them up to pitch.
At least it sets me free enough
to move on,
                    beyond the eddy stop,
into something I don't know.
Nothing counts for new.
I've spent it all on leisure —
In the end,
                    I know no trade.

The word I would like to say
will not come.
I am stuck alone.
I am my own betrayal,
but I am not wrong.
I am like the clouds which come each night,
and break
                    sometime.
There is a storm building,
but it is not great enough.
I have stood near,
but not near enough.
Showers come to pass
among the leaves.
Torn into little pieces —
the head and the gut.
All that is joy tears at us —

like rose thorns —
or bull briar:

Eastham, 1620    "that it did tear our very armour in pieces."
Thickets to fall in to —
Clearing away to it —
yet there are words —
words for all of this —
some I do not know —
some I dare not say
                (or sing.)
Keep silence, then, in place of lies.

A seal set on the day —
that the day releases —
opens only by ritual.
All men have known these words,
and most forget them.
We come up through magic,
but the magic leaves us.
Only a few strange old men remember,
alone in the midnight of their lives,
by smoking flames,
or what were lamps —
And they must guard the secrets,
that they do not fall into unaccustomed hands —
a common gold.
What could there be?
if all were adept —
apprenticed to the ore?
Ah, the clear eyes of early childhood.
Most cloud them.
They do not want it.

So that the music once known
is lost.
        Fingers still try for it,
but the head works tunings —
ugly masses of unpitched sound.
It is hard to come to the instruments —
our shame.
The secrets are no mysteries,
merely buried —
an accretion of rubbish,
but that rubbish is prized,

shards in museums. Dust.
Baggage we need not take with us,
yet fear to cut,
the habit, as grime, ingrained.

In chalice, in grail,
tulip or buttercup
-the holding flowers-
let them be the place
for substance, fragrance,
and the sound,
as instruments for sound,—
they bend along the wind.
What is hidden there
we need to know,
to lose our violence,
come up from that despair.
Do not pass by —
distill from dew —
that it may foam —
the hem of the robe heavy with it.
Agony, fear, eventually blood.
We move out many ways.
There is none better than another,
so that we look on things
as close at hand as flowers.
And a night with dry wind
-no rain or dew-
seals the cups.
The days will come —
                              with

or without us —
a past magnificence arise.
Mornings clear,
nights shine free.
A breath of wind is stirring
from the doldrums —
It is all straight enough —
the corners cut off
from themselves — the hanging thorns
parted.
Burst open, lost,

then nourished in the flood.
The music's there.
There is a place left
to pick it up.
The hard road softens,
planted to forests,
with aisles of silent memory,
and this return.
Coming, then, come over.
The last medium is not the last day.
And if that grail is found,
it will not be by search
-turned up in someone's garden
that it be known.
The rest of us be blessed,
and close the distance.


### C


In praise of
those who are crude among us,
and remain so,
Beatitude in wild places —
the cut off, and the rough edge —
raw against the schooled.
    Crafted —
               it is only in imagination
we receive refinement —
caries in the teeth,
             and too much sugar.
Colors bleed out to—
            into —
infusion, but it is no longer blood.
Call it imagination, then,
but it is scarcely that.
The flowers leach — — .

What would you change?
Where is the stem?
Will as will to change
**C.O.**    is constant —
            the newraw face

of the cliff.

　　　　　　To insulate is to destroy.
(Sheered, it will slide by —
the broken edges cohere.)
As of those few places
where a man stands sure,
the quantity remains uncooked.

Occurrence in blind saying,
let the sense come down,
　　　　　　　　　　and let it
pour,
　　　　finding its own levels.
What is there here?
beyond a mention?
　　　　　　　　or an answer?
hardly completed?
Tempted by the day,
get up into it.
There are no decisions —
it is all planned,
designed and temporary.
Where the wood breaks off
in a meadow —
an echo of voices, short and terse.

Watching the water,
and the rocks in the stream —
such polish, smooth sheering, it
occurs, but as roughness —
something to be undone tomorrow —
jagged splinters of ice.
A scream, highpitched,
a child's laughter.
Do not tamper with these things.
Interruptions
where they tend/fend
for themselves.
The business becomes complete.
Much to look into.
Hints here and there.
A darkening —
(After backing and filling

-three days of it-
slant rain from the west —
a good spin of it —
drifting.)
A movement, and its grace —
but was it learned?
Tell me its place:
The schools.
                   Ha!
Mention it, or do not.
I've climbed a distance
wondering why —
not out of a manual.
A health and a toast —
there is that mother ore
moves crude within us.
They are breaking to get in —
to get out again —
it may not happen after.
There is no precedent.

Call me. I will answer,
even come, if there is need.
But do not lecture.
I am deaf —
and the world is deaf, too,
to it.

However one touches,
the touch returns,
and it is not given.
Whatever is touched bends to
and away.
There is nothing makes a single force.
Rebound or redound.
Complete?
          It *was* complete.

We have done nothing.
Come to it fresh —
the unsettled source.
Who will find it?
Who will ask to find?
Complaint or compliant —

even the words,
various in themselves,
are set.
            The meanings come home,
all to the same nest.
The agonies are false.
Earth has none.
Yet we cling to them,
not quite double entendre,
but on the way.
It brightens, but only by lightning,
illuminates a moment,
then winks out.
The scaffold, built high,
will take a few at a time,
eventually all of us.
Only the untouched remain,
and men are not that.
Few other things,
but we will look for them,
sorting the rubble from rebellion.
It is there.
It does not hide,
lurking, in praise of — — .


## CI

The spirit enters —
no entrance way.
Vanishes another —
the entered into.
Love, as the spirit,
raises power,
pervades —
            a seamless lock.
Two hands — ten fingers.
Despite, there is
            always
a knot in the rope —
to squeeze an entrance.
Garotte.

No breath.
"bat er Fá."
Not too hard too take
from the Norse —
spells out its doom.
(or ours)
Useless, if the spirit does not,
will not,
                enter.
The lines cross, or hang empty:
Knot in the rope.
Do not bind —
the power is powerless,
flows by secret way/hatch,
underweigh.
Now, all that hangs outside
is the color of darkness —
no color at all.
The spirit is the power —
has none of its own.

Raise to the place,
fall fallow.
It is the fist
at the end of an arm.
Nothing in itself —
floating over.

On the walk — midsummer:)

River, run too full,
the bank will not have
you again.
Carried downstream,
a dry year's ghosts
rattle a few stones —
the air — the spaces.

Anonymous, well, try it
without the naming —
some of it will go —
others slip past.
Fixed, as the kiss might be —
the mood of a shower
enough to wet the dry stones.

But the great sound pretends —
take it from a surge —
let it go from that.
Wonder in a small glass.
Flashes —
            count them.
Space is more than space —
less —
there is no weight —
nor need.
Emotion is *a* motion
away — it carries
the center from itself.
It has no fear or gladness.
The spirit is more than spark.
Animus, whatever,
(is it life?
            Flowing
and gone
            out.)
There is a tension in it,
yet not tense.
Relaxed, it will not fall
or sleep.
It belongs to the other,
and the other is no measure.
As we are used —
used to it.
Spends itself —
nothing to spend —
flexion — no flux.
Needs little of us —
nothing in a size.

That it may change abruptly,
little question.
Pity and love will find themselves
in or outside.
Make motion again.
The quiet in the morning,
after the first chores,
mindless and silent —
alone —

first things done and
cleaned with the dishes,
a time to open up,
thick on the edge of breathing —
quiet enough to hear a pulse
beat
        something separate from the heat.
There is a thing in these,
but it may not be
what we are after.
The loose skein of the day
will tumble it soon enough.
Take stock —
an inventory of the soul —
that there is nothing there,
yet something sold.
Away from the heat of it
a plan.
Great change or charge of the morning,
*that* flux.

A time to check the levels —
water bursting over the dams —
smooth and oiled and dark.
It may not count for much.
It may.
Carried away in the clutter,
there is hope yet,
and we sing it —
all of these dark days.
Spring out —
a level trap.
The names are forgotten —
something carved on trees,
where the ice jam struck them
last winter.
Trace it — a rune language —
something to find out.
It becomes a parody of itself —
silences the spirit —
or the spirit leaves.

Complacent as the stars
seem that — and cold —

(are not
       is not)
there is time yet —
so much, and more —
and it is not counted out.
The specie is its own concern.
Ah, spirits, all.


## CII

Light makes an angle —
corners and boxes it.
It is a familiar — .
Is it?
Go in there?
Fears are not for it,
nor for us —
only for those
           we have brought with us.
May we break love or bread
in the making?
How to go in
         -evening-.
Oh evening, open it.
Evening come to me —
let me come to you. — )
Angle, corner, box — .
Trail off and away.
The agonies are now/always.
Where we fear, but not go in.

How to come back
         in?
Light makes *the* angle.

These last days —
to speak of them is not
to speak of tragedy —
tragedy is everywhere —
joy is well.
Inform both of them with love —
that love is the only informant —

a devotion and fidelity,
something that will not move
unless it moves itself —
where the act and the life
are one
            and cannot be broken
without loss to both of them.

It is only at the height of knowing
that we speak so —
a clouded knowing in sharp light.
Fear that the journey was unsettled —
that the power has gone,
or that it was not power.
What it seemed to be:
The double blade of harvest
and at quick.
Grasp, but the grasp is not ours.
There must be love in it.

At times, my love,
the fingers ache
-extreme-
            an arc-
their touch to yours.

At time, and times become
the only time —
regret and change.
Oh, pull it in —
a gaff to land it —.
No, another term,
a love that will not term
no matter what its place,
or angle,
            sensing.
Let it breathe —
and I must go, and you,
a mist — a place of tears.
That is the dream,
                        the actual.
I cannot reach it in another place.
It comes through you,
its quietness, and

gentle holding.
Do not ignore it:
That,
              in the spaces —
—all that comes between —
love is a brutal thing.
It is gentle only as it touches.
Die with, or die without.
We surely die.
All of it appears to be —
no more, no less.
                        Whatever is.
The surface is a depth of it.
We do not see the surface,
looking in for more.
As very stones that sweat —
the heat around them —
-pivot/touch-
the light comes back —
the heat its purity.
The light through darkness
to the edges.
                  Transpose
another color.
Here, as it happens,
out of fear.

"that we are all, each of us,
                                    different

**Ed Verzyl**      and *that* is the gap,
                                    in touching,

but not age.
the measure of experience is
                                    doing."
Opens the door.
"time,
**ibid.**          things,
                        will."
Rather than to stand alone
on the hill
looking down —
                        contempt
in that aloofness.
Now time.

A placement on the page.
Angle *to* the light,
                    and the edges bleed —
their sharpness
                    that angle
of light.
            (The tool fractures itself.
The light is chrysalis —
pupa dries —
                    spreads wing.)
It is *this* place —
                    no other
Ideas flee the actual.
All that I put into it withers.
The place remains.
                        Ruminating on
a stalk of hay:
I cannot wear these things well —
and there are times when nothing comes
of them, or of anything.
There is no 'else.'
It is the brood of spirit —
brooding.
                    It is no eagle — but alone.

The tensions,
            let them be
stress for stress,
those which flex to a crossing
current.
" — the true test of a bridge.
Rigid is not firm."
                        (I breaks there.)
            resilience.

**Ed Verzyl**                        " — — a bridge
connects the shores, but
                            does not
make them one."
Span and span
                    in light
lights up
                again
the angle.

## CIII

Suppression:
        And what it is to suppress
self for another —
            not to interrupt —
come at the right times.
(Green of the hills —
a certain light — the sward.
A certain rightness.
Come — come out.

In the morning
I have called for rain,
and the rain has come, and
passed over.
I have looked for the light,
and the light has shone even
with darkness.
I have planted a seed, and
the flower has opened,
and fallen.
I have walked far enough,
moved nothing.
            Stood still.
(And the view of the hills —
green green green
comes out
        -a journeying-
Enough.

To suppress only those things
which are harmful.
To remember
        all of the uses —
to reject what is unfit.
If it does not fit that other
no matter how it may lie in my hand.
To let loose
        in the lightening of air
the good that surrounds:
The smile of the rain and
the smile of the fire —

smile in the face of the flower —
even the agony in smiling.
What counts.
(The hills in their green, and
the fullness of ripening — — —
smoke.

Slow,
      in their distance and time,
the images —
             given for love.
Keepsake and talisman —
a beauty clings to them —
an aura —
yet life is removed.
Whatever I give you,
it is not
      more than
not enough.
It is the image,
and you, in your dress,
are alive,
      as the hills
are alive.
      Can we not
go there?
      Is it nostalgia
that I remember
          such times as we have?
or a reaching for such
          as may be?
A touching of branches —
the trees in the wind.
(In surfeit of being
some leaves fall
        green.

The words are in wounds,
and the wounds heal
        slowly.
What have we done?
        or not?
Done is the doom of it.
Sounds with such clangor —

the doors of confinement
where we have kept and suppressed
what should have been open.
(Free range of the hills —
an opening green.

Bind up, if you will,
and I,
          in the girding,
as struggle will have it —
leave struggle
                    behind us.
Angels are messengers —
let them be as they will be —
— live —
and that is all that is holy.

Let me in bed,
                    or out of it,
come to you —
                    life in the coming,
speak to you —
                    hold to you —
measure no end
                    to the entrance.
There is no image
                    left of it.
It is itself,
          and we are.
Than open the windows —
let in the light and the frost,
and the darkness and heat.
Come to the hills
                    and the green,
with me,
          come.
And in your distances,
lone and alone,
at the moments of loneness.
Love is no word.
Let it not wound.

          bless you

keep you
Such benediction —
no saying.
The hills, in their green.
We can
go out.


**CIV**

In this —
washed scale of the morning
-quiet now- —
I do rise up again,
stretch toward the window
(night has left it,
and the cobwebs in the grass
face up.)
I was always one for mornings.
Though I have forgotten them
at times,
this one reaffirms.
I turn back to where you lie
still sleeping,
and a smile in sleep
is worth this morning.
I am happy here
with you —
whatever nighttime rains
washed
clean
away.
What else the night has brought us
stays in dream,
and a remembrance.
It is ours.
Need not say it.

Keep.
Receiving/giving,
both are one
(They change their faces —
now and again

                              from *me*
from *you*
                *to* me
*to*.you.)
It is fixed in change —

**casting the I Ching**  is the open book of changes.
**9/10/76**  Whatever found there,
                              let us take
what forms a use.
                              It is good to do that.
When the times hang ripe,
fruit reddens in the dark.

Come with me.
                As you sleep,
come here.
                These states of being,
all of them,
                are one place, and
we divide them hastily
with no purpose.
Let us put them close together
where the edges fit.
Stones make the pattern.

We have survived it all.
There is love in this place —
                              in this room.
It is not needed that all things
should be reciprocal.
                At times we scatter them
to remake.
                There are those places
-distances —
we cannot join.
Learn peace, and waiting.

Doubt is an honesty.
holding, and holding to.
This,
        in the night,
that touch which brings us
in
        to each other,

into —
        a connection closer than bone or blood,
releases,
        fleshes us in sleep.
How may it come about?
Only as the morning opens
do we know the tempers
of these metals,
                hardening to the stroke —
the hinge which widens from its pivot,
but is still the hinge.

Despair may seize us
in its hands,
                and by the throat;
but that was in the night,
and this is morning.
One times one.
Divide it,
        take away,
replace,
        diminish,
we cannot.
The surety of what it is
-tread down or flowing-
what *we* are.
There is no other being
than this being,
                ours,
our bodies in this space
these spaces.
                Changed
it may be, as the change is
changeless.
Entering on dream,
raise up this morning,
raise it from the dream
-its dream-
do we hold the sunlight
in our hands,
                or do the eyes
shoot fire from that source?
What season is it?

Whose reality?
          or being?

I came in here as another man,
and you another woman.
We cannot guess ourselves
from whom we were, or
whom we may become.
Nor how we may go out
                    again.
I am looking through the window,
yet I look far back —
at you —
          just stirring.
Have you heard me?
Only through this silence,
when the pulse rides in the ear,
can you hear it.
It is not gainsaid in speaking.

Outside, the leaves are turning,
but that is only color.
In this life the many colors
merge and break away —
and come again —
                    and break away — —
I have asked too many questions.
Still, that is better than one answer
given
          to nail us shut.
I'll go downstairs, and see
what may have changed.
If the night dealt well with us,
by its own lights,
and by the shadows from the moon.
Some chill hangs stagnant.
Smoke.
          Some regrets.
Look back upstairs,
but that is not a backward look.
The sun that warms me here
is there with you.
The morning centers.
Ah, breathe in the morning.

I hear you stir again.
Look out.
       This clarity:
Dew lasts long.
The autumn sun
          is rising


## CV

"Is this
       all of it?"
A question.
         Count me questions —
an affirmative —
          no answer.
All.
     At one close angle
years mean nothing.
We do not come to the end of it.
(Of them.)
Scanted,
        it brings on restlessness,
to do what cannot be known
            to do.
To end with energy wasted —
turning circles in a road —
eternal 360's,
and no way out of it.
Many have gone there,
pulling at the vortex —
heading further down,
hearing, clearly,
the screams of the damned —
their own in chorus.
It must center in this room,
grow old, if need be.
There is little else outside,
unless the room is known,
and, further,
        loved.
(An old man walks here.
He was young once,

                    but only

in his oldness.
*IT* —
        and I, this man,

am scared of *it.*
Sheer size —
                its weight —
oh bring me weights
to counterbalance —
                        no,
not the imperative.
I live here well enough.
Get up and go outside,
                        in season.

There is a smell this fall
                        of leaves —
leaves decaying:
                spiritus frumenti —
and it is a similar
                (leaves smelled this way
years ago)
            this season.
Some might pass on that.
I cannot.
        I am here,
still here,
            and not that differently.

Yet,
    the slight turn —
turning leaves
            over.
old-
    old-
Cast the accounts.
It is a similar —
                no sameness.
Smell —
        hangs.
Thin the air for it.
Haze hanging —

strung out above me
                        on the hills.

old-
        old-
I can hardly believe that,
and yet I must believe it —
believe the question —
take its mark as echo —
the answer always here —
a tragedy embalmed.

I came in from an immediacy —
perhaps the first smoke of winter
on my breath.
I looked again.
It was not easy.
There were figures in that room —
dead figures and live ones —
but there were times
                        when I could not tell
one from the other.
I had heaped my questions
in the corners —
over everything —
                        books and papers
scattered —
                        but there might have been
another music.
And all that/all this.
There was a life there —
in its presence.
I sat down and waited.
Could we bring ourselves
to know more of it?
Or was it *only* my
                        self?
yours — a fiction?
or between us — tissue
that forever sealed us off
from each other?
In some sense —
                        my things —

many other
              dimensions.
Oh, then, I asked,
(and it is not granted to ask —
wrested from iron —
pulling the hinge bolts through —
a splintering.)
It was a close way —
always a close way — closed.
'Is this all?'
Despair,
              and that clutter —
or *that* even neatness —
*this* dust and strewing
for a life.
If it is the woman here,
let us go up quietly to bed
-in the darkness-
quickly.
And I will enter her,
fucking for the sheer joy of it —
no object between.
Hopefully,
              fucked in return —
a double tenderness unthought.

Polish of the moonlight
streaming in here
                        -cold-
but the leaves still hung —
blow wild against it.
It is not excitement of the light,
and yet it seems to be.
I will go down.
Release my girl —
a madness on my face
-moon madness, in a lunar month,
and the madness of intervening
                                    leaves —
their tempering.
All of them,
          or it.
My face is in that swoon —

that stitch of utterance.
The words will not cohere there —
or not in patterns that we know.
(but it is not always the business
of words to do a bidding —
they have sure lives
                    in other places.)
The questions come out
other questions —
sadness or delight.
Bring all to pleasure.
*Bring* delight — —.

###################

A wet branch switching —
all the night
against the night —
its drops of moisture.

                ###################

A wind, new rising —
on the ridges —
over
        and gone.

                ###################

Far off, the sea —
two waves in cross rip
slap
        contending.

                ###################

A red cast in the moon
is dust,
            and here
no moon's affair.

                ###################

All — All of it.
It is that faintness given outline.
Come in from journey.
Rest.
            Easy.

All to all.


## CVI

But who, and what
in such a light?
no sight —
            the blinding
make of it;
this dark — a cave —
a cold within the clouds.
Impersonal as
fish swim/bird fly —
time of it.
The outerness,
                    and in.
Small world below —
its dizziness.
Intense, as only silence
is intense, and knowing
broken for the knowing it.
Blood sound in the ears —
a faint wind at the draw.
Around is road enough,
and sound is sight —
the same blood passing
through the eyelids
                    caught
in light — these cloud
                    skeins
solid for the touching them —
a stepping down.
No passing through,
the space is all of it —
and opening beyond
                    is
space - an all way space.
As palpable to touch,
impervious —
the space of objects
                    touched

and handled.
                    Faint remembrance —
but the scent of memory
stays close to earth.
It cannot rise in cold.
Its furies — volatile —
cannot burn.
It is nothing, and no matter
of that nothing.
Return to light —
in such return
a rising
                geared and pressured
in and over —
make one presence felt
and heard.
It is no darkness —
yet it would be —
eyes accustomed to obscurity —
see well.

A tension — raised —
its many sources
                    raised
(Ice and hail precede
the rains of summer.)
Conjuring —
                and no mere magic.


What are we about?
A first intrusion —
men upon this scale of being.
When did *I* appear
                    among others?
Forget that quickly —
                    sliding scale

across the sun
                or
such as touches it —
cool shower in parched season.
Whatever was it?
It did not face well.
Only the scale —

such fingers leaving prints
in sand,
          or is the sand
a cloud held
            shading?
Peeping of the sun

through
            shadow *after* shade.
When it is —
trails/
        /quietly
a vapor.
Now and again — reform it.
Reify —
        and such a word
in such rare space.
Not the *out* or *in*
              side

holds.
      Let it
hold on.
(An embarrassment —
the sense of blood rush —
the rank of blood —
            its rise.

Take, oh take
again - the flowering.

Flowing well,
it all flows.
Cannot in such places
look for more than
mere words —
BUT IT WRESTLES IN THE WIND.
Take me — carefully —
away.
      Intrusion once
again. It rises,
and the bare foot of the day
kicks a hole in it.
(Bare fact.)
First shaft,

for some the prima luce —
(Did they think of it?
more than rise?
that facet of it?
Let it all be.
And I am wrenched away.
My sense of it:
Do I belong?

Certain things that I need —
that I would take or give.
It is
        a given credence.

Only among these clouds
that freedom —
looking —
        gently looking.
I am outside.
Sen
    ten
        tious.
(One cloud could, breaking,
mark resemblance
                to it.
And when the rising
was a distance
scattered over us —
the archetypes confused —
their arches difficult —
remote from what we knew,
yet, closer, made a confidence —
a pact with fortune.
Oh remembrance
                (earth again)
do not break the faith.
In this, a final bourne —
the situation of our unity,
a strength.
        The test of solid landscape,
cloud on cloud.

## CVII

We were cast like stones —
like dreams
                    our casting.
Be it like or unlike
common sense —
we cast about it.
But we were whole and primal.
In our compassing
John Gill          we cast the dream.
9/23/76          What was it like?
that casting?
Speak only from the pivot
-that one ground-
                              the self —
its symbols.
C.G. Jung          If I take your hand,
I know only what I feel.
You are veiled
                    (my vision of you)
where were you cast?
(Whatever you have seen or heard
or felt in other ways —
it will come back,
                    after it has gone
a season —
                    cast
like a stone.

It is the air around us —
                              clear
and formed —
                    an air
that whistles after stones —
their casting.

Of certain things, the whole,
                              (no part)
I bring to you the bearing —
absolute, as nothing is
outside reality.
                    Perfection

464

never touches them at root.
The edges cloud and blur,
and what is sharp seems soft.
No use!
And I would bring you things to use
-tools-
         as knives or scissors —
spoons and shovels.
                Axe
to strike the wood and split it.
You must stand confused,
                no help.

Reaching out to me —
it is as clear for you,
             but I am
lost in fog — for grasping.
Dim shapes of what we are
pass and repass across the windows,
screened and contained.
              Is it night?
We tell each other that it is,
but it is several:
           Night for you,
as night for me —
the sight — the whole of it —
stands by and waits.
That may be where it lies.
To wait — that patience —
that utter bondage.
The whole speaks through us,
and we are nothing more than instruments.
The stones keep whistling —
(or is it wind and stones?
"Say what ye lyst, it will not be

**Anne Bolyn**    Ye seek for that cannot be found."

A view is overview —
a heterodyne, and too much
seen —
         passed or repassed.
I drop
         into the blood of the year —
an autumn blood:

465

             this stream.
The blood contained/
              contains another.
I am only one —
         and I see little —
feel less —
those things, and only those
which are around me for my use.
Cast out like stone —
            one stone.
I seek.
      It cannot be found.
A thought continuing!
Let them come
as long as they will.
The day — opening — ?
Let the dark.

No one can.
        *All* can.
The hiatus in such a day —
simply to see an old man
once more before he dies.
Oh, the pity of it.
Perhaps we should not.
Sit quietly, or go
A place he would have liked.
Old eyes flickering —
smile — a little remembrance,
Why do we do it?
any of it?
Misery of other years
           foisted
on this one —
        let it out.
The rise of it
cast like stones again.
There is a hurt
no man need give
nor should.
Wounds are gratuitous
in themselves.
A hurt may cleanse —

**John Grant**
**10/6/76**

466

let it fall as hurt —
no more.
We presume upon ourselves —
end in a place of skulls
or stones.
The darkness of such thinking!
Much that is,
                    remains in dark,
and yet it is not all of it —
or even such as makes
a greater part.
Whatever then, holds up
is, in itself,
only what itself may be.

Cast me no stones.
Cast out no man.
All have their own conceits —
resting places —
stones in a wall.

Well in the dark —
I rise against it,
a night among moon nights —
to walk through such fields.
All fields are open.

In no note too much,
that things level themselves.
We are with them.
Ah, to be with.
It is that supportive.
You with me.
I am with you.
Cast no stone.
(There are two of them.)
Either breaks —
                    wipes the other
out.

Looking one day
                    (this will do)
to the upper reaches,
the mountain over my shoulder —
I see —

well,
            what *do* I see?
I touch so little.
The flow of clouds,
and that mountain.
Flow of a tide —
            a sea
in other times,
other works
            (worlds)
But it is the mountain
stone and solid —
            cast.

I have held out my hand —
to such mountains as this one —
who has not?
(Few know what they have done.
Do I?
It is a wavering sound —
(an echo?)
It is a wall —
(wavering?)
Move up that side!
And the anger grows.
What do we put here —
in its stead?
A hand held light —
that wavering,
            echo,

until the wall is reached
lean against it —
            out of breath —
cast there, but steady.
The reflection will blur
or change outside it.
The sea change:
Athwart?
By the board?
Who has heard it?
            in that guise?
So much, and on to it forever.

The doom defended —
writ or deed.
Cast in that fashion,
The directions shake out,
and we are taken there
Cast no man or stone.
Alive/
          /arise
in pure air.


## CVIII

Per gloria ad gloriam —
To make a note of it
-that line or thread —
measurable, but
                    unobtrusive.
Come in here —
                    absolve it.
Nothing beyond the self to praise,
or blame —
                    a little of it
left —
          that glory in a touch.
A sparkling — break of spark —
leap flame
                    leapt.
Grasp for the rise,
a lightness,
                    to reach,
make and reach
                    once more.
But what comes through?
what thoroughfare?
Reverse it — and rise once more.
The evening.
                    All night at the table.
Timbrel — sound lightsome —
instruments of age —
and no age differing.
Sing loud — or loud enough —
and echo it —

but echo is not heard aright —
A fault in sound.

There is a breeze blows west —
follows the sun —
                    that transit.
Shadow will subside at noon —
the overhead
                fall.
Afternoon's the best of it.
It goes lighter,
as one learns the path
among stones.
They hold the heat of it,
(oh,
        later in the night
when wind has struck the frost in
where.
            A ritual for blindness
follows me.
What do I know?
If I am now known —
nothing — fond indulgence —
mere blowing and sucking
of the thumbs.
When I was younger, and
in those many shadows,
I was close as now —
                    another side
to what I'd chosen,
what had chosen me.
I step down early,
and I step down late
                    or later —
measuring by what I have
                        (or leave)
A poor way into it.
Man's measure is adjunctive —
personal —
baggage and possession
possess him.
Later and further
the greatest tree

(so named by him)
a blade of grass.

Per gloria  ad —
we move through doom,
and move away again.
The grouping —
how we marvel —
take our words
and bend them into follies —
misconceptions —
coincidence and the like —
and do not see —
and cannot see.
Measure as a step —
oh moving measure.
It is not likely —
already past the heats
this afternoon.
Flash out —
                    flash by flash,
what could be written of it,
and no seam left —
no place for seam —
little writing that may be done.
The canyon walls
go dark —
                    the sun's warmth
waning out of them.
Illusions where it is so,
innocence?
                    appalling ignorance,
and wicked at more places
than we know:
                    The seams.
Pocket and cul de sac —
a rumpling.
I have had to say it,
and to feel its saying —
coming back and on the way.
Have your will,
and take your way.
Picking among hills and bones,

looking for artifacts —
those most broken
                              prized —
patched.
What the elders had thrown out,
forgotten.
Swallow a pinch of dust,
there is no water here
-cold dust-
and that for sustenance.
When I have hammered long enough,
on good reason, there will be
something for marvelling
                              -unravelled-
the learned text.
Good reasons falling
by the board.
Take away the reasons
in this time —
these last drawn shadows.
Way again.
I came in here
to brighten —
leave the shadows,
but the shadows follow.
Take your sense of it —
youth and the sap of it,
and I'm impoverished
                              duly.
All of this as those.

The glories, oh the glories,
let them rise again,
but where or what —
no leading and no following.
I know these places.
Stasis follows movement,
movement stasis,
moving.
Puff of dust —
the smoke —
in valleys
still the falling —

falling
       to the head of the draw.


## CIX

Of the age in which they live —
arbiter — criterion.
They will leave no artifacts —
little to handle or wonder at —
the high cliffs barren —
no glyph.
Artifacts — no baggage.
The junk proliferates,
broken and flawed —
hardly a sound bone
                left.
The dust through ribs —
those spaces —
         eyes —
what were — and lost — themselves.
The terrible and wise
lie hidden.
It is not a single man's journey,
yet each man, singly,
           tries it,
and assays his weight against it.
Loses weight —
the substance in his footprints.
Oh lead me in
        and out of it.
I have a little space before,
and still behind me,
but that will swallow
in a darkness beyond —
lost to lights and heats.
And I have been here before,
long ago,
      some salt
or lime
      underlying.
There will be one way in —
one to stay.

I do not go out.
What do I leave?
guano on a cliff?
Sea island, where a wind blows
constant —
                one direction.
(Reaching high to pierce it —
smoke ring tenuous.
It vanishes —
                stale as smell —
a wraith in that smoke.

But to look,
                one might find graffiti
some time hence.
Propping the wall,
                        these koans:

'The life is various — not disparate.'

'To show you
that I know
                where I am —
who you are —
I love you.  I love you.'
'The simplest words are,
                                always,
the right ones.'

Stiffened by wind,
the hide of the matter
clotted —
                darkest of blood.
Remove it —
cut through the tangle —
little else remains,
and it will fail
                eventually.
Uncomfortable to the end of it —
oh the stiffness of that wind.

In comfort, to sit close,
the fire alive and beyond
the bounds,
Darkness of a world wellstridden —

what does, and does not hold
together.
Coherence is not all of it,
but a part that will shape,
and some of that shape
comes out as evil.
We have spent our time
correcting and supporting —
shoring a building
which may not deserve the effort.
No bad thing to begin again
from nothing but the ground
upon which we stand —
watch the other drop
in its own decay,
untended and unloved,
as it cannot support our love
in being.
Well, that's last,
and time is lost with it.
The rest is culch —
kitsch — a rottenness of soul.
Bad taste — too tame for censure.
Bland as dishwater,
                dull,
it cannot catch the light,
and rarely will touch fire.
No artifacts —
a few names in his story,
but hardly meriting that —
to be forgotten early.
No. Let it be, at that point.
Nerve and muscle opening.
My mind is strong enough for that.

(I came in one door,
left by another —
a sure sign of company —
possibly today?
Was this what I had in mind?
I doubt if I can pull further
than a bit at a time.
   Still that door

(doors)
-both open-
that the breeze blows through them —
front and back.
I've talked it over with myself —
few others to talk to.
They shake their heads.
Think on this or that —
but few of them will do that —
much or little.
Heading out —
if the coast is clear.
Take this little —
shards and stellae —
    bury them out of the way,
    that later they may be found.
    The source will not be known.
    I will lie silent.


## CX

I remember:
               a small store
in a small town.

**Chatham, Mass.**   There may have been two stores
perched between towns.
One was called 'Lake's' —
the other had no signboard —
a family operation.
I never went into either one.
(A possible reflection —
that these were poles —
mirrored —
             the same place.)
But there was a sense of being —
poise —
        history implied —
that the stores remained
after the neighborhoods they served
had disappeared —
islands of the past

faced on a highway.
I went my way past them,
thinking of other things,
but those grey buildings have survived
in mind's eye.
I still think of them,
wondering,
                    did I need their presence?
Was there nothing inside
            something
which I should have known —
should be had.
Daily I move in similar ways —
and daily pass on.
There are other concerns
that jostle the signposts —
let these remain in the stream,
along a skein.
It is unwise to cut the thread.

Assorted —
                    colors of all sorts
in boxes —
                    heaped on shelves.
An order —
but such an order
as cannot be seen easily
to hold.
            A logic
beyond neatness —
something other than a man's.
Next — drop the philosophy.
Ideas, the best of them,
amount to nothing.
People do,
                    separate and bleeding.
Individuals.
Masses turn sour.
The aggregate is worth nothing.
And bare the sky,
as bare the way.
Bar!
Come close to all of this,
but resist.

Let us know where.
Where have *you* been?
Why was it you?
(Now the sky is deepening,
for want of dark)
but the clouds of dark
are moving —
after a dark day.

Now the rise of light,
if it is sun or other.
I salute you, day —
there, by symbols
along the route.
Colors in a desert,
or water there,
in a waterless place.
It is a time to feast —
fatten for the lean shadows
far ahead.
We will be taken there.
(Purchase at the store
                    unvisited?)
All of my time
-ours-
in choices —
but choices come unbidden —
unnoticed.

Expanses returned.
That *will* be noticed.

There must be other points —
sparks to keep it going.
A suspension —
something solid to rest on —
the day will not crumble,
no matter what is broken ·
against it.
There are times
                    axiomatic
in some of them — a reach
-a climb-
a scrambling up dry valleys.

This was what we came to?
past those stores?
(A glass of coca-cola
to cheer us —
or nothing.
Regard the roadside spring.
It was a source,
but sources run dry —
no notice
unless a man sees
the final flood before
the water goes.
                    It
leaves, first, a stain on the sand
-ripple marks —
and then nothing.
I am uncertain of all this,
but I keep to it —
put on blinders,
that I do not confuse myself
in variety.
Those things a man cannot
take in
            lest he faint or fall —
dulled.
The next man may.
(I did well to reject the stores,
see none of it.
Now I may regret its theory,
but I have more.)

These are the things:
Portents and pointers.
I live in one small place.
That there is another?
Well, straighten it.
Paths are cumbered,
men on them,
                    cumbersome.
The roads and memory
dense as thickets.
Look to the star
                    and go.

## CXI

Nor will the current
                  tolerate a bridge
-none to withstand its wash-
high water, or the stream.
Moves as an instance of its own
                       predicament,
passing, in the night,
                a rivulet
turned later into vein and nerve —
the land surrounding, breathes by it.
Caught —
            the flow may once subside,
but briefly, ploughs its margins
where the forests were —
new channels and washed sand.
(The bars hold ripple marks
long after, as a wandering tide,
the fitful, certain breaking of a rhythm —
we do not see the whole of it.
Reaches out to it by vector or valence —
the words for it {distilled as
                {distorted
what flows beneath it.
(Men see nothing but the movement —
movement, constant, will remove the fact
before the fact is actual.)
Fossil of one life — shard of another —
downstream eddying the power
and what moves against it,
bruised on stone — the fact —
sweat at the shoulder —
follow the constant stars —
the day and night of them —
their moving, too, another moving.
What were the guideposts —
marks on old deeds —
                    tall trees —
as marked — heaped cairns —
all washed away — there is no memory
long enough to say the whole.
The scent of forests lasts

but little longer.
and the current threads another way.
The scent of water?
                    Who will find it?
What the water bears:
                    Ceaseless water.
In the end, it ceases, too.

Of the particular
                    instance
when a flash flood
rose over one bank
a little faster than it did
along the other —
swept the moorings free,
and took away the bearing timbers,
set them, like a keel,
mainstream.
The rest shuddered and followed.
Downstream, it beached
on rocks.
Helpless and useless,
the raw edges of its abutments
open again,
as distant as they had been.
Never joined, but once,
an illusion (bridge)
fought a way through these —
a transverse current.
Maimed and weak —
as oak is straw,
transitory as we are —
our idea of bridging.
(Here, it's in the plans.)
Nothing will last longer
than the wake of the ferry
plying.
(Darkening, darkening,
the edges foam.

The motive power, gently be seen,
wears at the stone,
and grows at the root —
bayous, left shrinking and rising,

left dying — the ponds and swamps,
and the land — other forms of it.
Far sounds in the valley,
the water removing its course,
and the bridges lain idle,
such as remained
in the flood seasons.
We might pass over
to a land with no passage.

That the stream becomes sign,
fire sign
          and thirst,
land sign
              and mountains.
Sea sign
          and deep.
In the end it becomes
merely itself —
that there are no symbols
other than actual.
The bridge becomes desperate,
returns to itself — its components.
From the logs and the planks
come rot and decay —
a mold in the forest.
It will come again:
A generation of trees,
and no symbol.
Signed in the blood of this world,
a sign in a sunset.
The bloodlight refracted
-caught in the dust-
that the worlds of energy
and those of this structure
mingle before darkness.
No bridge,
and a hard world leaves
in that of the sound,
and the sound.

Blind us in colors,
deafen in music —

these are for heat
and for silence.
Couple and strengthen
for place into place:
The risk, and the bridge.


### CXII

Come, give me the lights.
I will carry the flames in my hands.
burning myself on coals,
but never these fires unbidden.
A place to recognize — may it
all be such a place.
I know no way into it
save by art — a sanity
in this, an unstable world.
Such cognizance in music
-that clear ordering-
the forms and focus of music,
what the music dictates at beginning.
How good that we do not order it
ourselves! That no one can.
No thing can create it —
a sui generis.
A telling — a tolling.
(The hands stray slightly —
the fire misgiven —
and yet that remembrance
comes pure.

In the madness of one season,
not itself,
but what we were about
                              in it.
that sanity
               -not stasis-
it strikes different each time —
pulls toward the light
as the light fractures.
(The fact, upon its feet,
removes.)

Fire and seed —
                    that some seed
lies dormant —
**Piñon pine**                    possible only
in heat.
It singes into life.
That which gives, by simulacrum,
poised
            -its pivot-
takes away.
                    My hands ache,
blistered,
                    where the fire ran.
And I am here
                    suspended
**Wisconsin River, at Stevens**    I talk into myself
**Point, Wisconsin,**                    -by a river-

**10/30/76**    -in it — on rock island.
I watch the water — a dark flange
stained with darkness,
as the fire of this day
obscure it —
                    a fall migration
overhead.
Shadow on the river more real than they are,
and what I hear of life
more alive than life itself.
A spirit casts no shadow,
no echo of its voice,
but that is lore and
absent from the fact.
Reflect — reflect it.

(Coin in leaves,
windrow of poplar's, and
harsh wind —
the creak of it —
crew on the island.
            ********************

Broad face or bosom,
open/flow/down/
river silence

484

post meridian.
Light in here:
that warmth again.
Bread as the sun is —
peasant stamp.
Never shatter,
                    then balance.
Alone in a strange town.
The fear of nothing except myself.
(A cold wind blowing
against my hands.
Where I held flame,
only the dust
(specular iron)
of the earth.

**Duluth, Minnesota**
**10/31/76**

Close to the old bones,
so many close things —
eating the fish of the lake
the antediluvian life poised there.
In this town,
                    as this town is —
settling into a rhythm,
a slight change from others —
which is its own.
Fear in the early morning
-that grey-
should I go out?
Is there any place to go?
Away from here —
then *that* is here,
and there is nothing else to say of it.
Bruising myself on alien stones,
slight muscle tension —
tendon pulls.
I am afraid of nothing but myself.
There is little left —
life saps low enough —
but it moves forward.
                              On.
Enough of all of this —
and I cry for fire
                    once again.

Redoubt of sorts —
over the hill-a music-
other than the life here.
Words take off unbidden —
history and theory.
It is nothing then —
falling
          the complete plomb —
line held fast and taut
ın the wind.
(A pig of lead attached to it.)
I do not direct this —
useless as an old ship
listing on a tide ledge.

Oh gentle, gentle being —
I would be there,
wherever, where.
But the light I carried
loses —
          lost by me?
It carried —
                only in itself —
whatever else might be.
Life picked it up,
whatever that was,
sound or sight occurs
                        regardless.

Wave, oh bring me
wavelength —
stir of rising —
there are other lives than mine
around us all —
but it is not selfish to ignore them.
What little else may be
brings pleasure
— to live outside —
but there is little of it
possible.

High watermark —
the ponds are full again.
In such times I shall be

a visitor —
solitary — listening —
a time for winter sleeping.


### CXIII

**Wittgenstein**

If you can say it at all,
there is a way with words
to say it clearly —
though the words themselves may
take the sense beyond your meaning,
clearer than you were, ever.
There *is* control,
                    but we do not.
An order,
              and we cannot.
If the eel slips through
-still-
        grasp it.
It is not the fault of the eel,
nor a bid for negligence.
Ah, too severe,
the rest of it is song —
that so the birds rise up
as numerous as dust —
motes that will come together
in a cloud —
                a storm's migration,

I drew a circle.
Where it held me in
I felt the chain —
no evil thing might touch me,
though evil festered
in the world around me.
I was blessed and cursed in this.
I built it for myself,
and the promptings came
                        unreal
and unused.
These words are dark,

and the way is dark,
and the round dance
danced at midnight
in the dark of the moon
under rain clouds.
(Clouds of spirits —
shadows of wings by day.)
And the cleft in the land
where the river ran —
blood in its channel —
stones for its words —
plain, all plain,
a saying.

Things best not said.
Bay on, and at the moon.
Do not attempt beyond the bonds.
We cannot insist upon
the word — the ritual —
or a performance of the word.
Its act lives on
                    inside a being.
So silent there.
And blood poured out —
the earth was bathed in it.
The heart dried and cracked
and died,
                and the earth died with it.
How do we say such things?
(Ah, the many names of God again,
and cannot find the godhead.)
Blood in the wood,
and water from stone.
We are on that way,
and then we are off
                    again
and again.
Move one step over —
return —
and more return —
the words piled higher
than the walls which house them.
Seed in the granary,

**Morton Marcus,**
**Aptos, California**
**11/11/76**

488

and yet the granary will open —
no doors to spill.
And all of this a motion,
wind across the plains —
evoking word from tree,
or from the blowing wind.
Ah, many times,
but many times return,
and do not go, and cannot.
Over the majesty of day or night,
these words,
                    cut and fitted —
yet we do not know that fit,
and cannot give it.
Few others, then,
but words,
                    and words obscure
as well as name,
a casuistry of law.
I do not know about it
more than what I know.
The word will clothe
and then disclose again.

What I have been working through
-a high design-
is sudden —
on the page is sudden.
Through the lip
a shout of doing —
and a pace in passing.
Words that grasp,
and move away with what they seize,
Not what we know of them.

Beyond all this,
what cannot be as said,
or cannot be
                    -at all-
a monstrous substance,
greater than its past or present,
leaving nothing but the wound to say
(and nothing said.)
Nothing aside —

or yet another motion,
shadow and the words
chill dead —
in such a darkness.
Roughened,
          as the edges may be
rough,
      yet bound
into that wind which blows
-no surcease-
let us move on,
over —
          heave
beyond
          abeyance.
Strike on words as stones,
the wash pebbles boiling
-tide's mouth-
further, what may be,
stones in chips
along the glacial edge —
words as morraine —
the high pitch —
however that angle may be —
something to bed down,
and not a dynasty
                    more exact.
It has been a way,
and yet the wave of it
far less
        as loss.
RAVE IN THESE WORDS — AND RAVEN!
It will be easier to talk
when splinters have dismantled
mountains —
                no more
shapes or sizes
which will not give more.
Perhaps- a less or more-
yet we will find it all.
Some day a picturing.
Let it not be picked at.
The soul will live its art.

No, we have no wisdom,
nothing such as those pure arts,
and more than Gods
who cannot find that morning,
or be given over to it.
An easy chipping —
as the sun will reach our window
in the morning,
                    and another, later,
but at angle —
                    tangent —
it can never be an opposite.

A sense leaks through —
but not a definition.
It is simplicity —
yet not the whole
which makes it simple.
Fluid, plastic,
it is left behind us.
Take little.
Word for word —
the saying is.


## CXIV

I took,
        into myself,
a property not my own.
A confidence in what
I could not have.
                    I did, now, know you,
dared think of you —
and laid these stones on air.
When such things fell and vanished,
I was alone again —
but you *were* there.
(The trust comes later.
Of who? Of whom?)
The first time then
-no puppet on my strings-
I touched you —

                          from my distance
into yours.
                    I felt a pressure —
prescience - ourselves -
and me.
I cannot know, now or ever,
how the signs reciprocate,
or what your will
can make of mine.
A clasp of elements
does not lose track,
or blur identities.
How simple.
                    All we do not know.
Cannot go anywhere to be alone
and should not.
(But of that property
there must be a synthesis,
something we did not have
as proper —
                    now a thing
made plain and ours —
an attrition —
                    towards the dying in the sun —
to leave behind.
(A trail of spoor.
                    An army follows.)
And yet this property —
how little or how much of it —
it makes small difference,
and it will not hold.
All that I claim from what has lain
dropped along the road —
a use for me —
yet not my own.
A hard time searching,
here or back,
so many threads to draw —
be drawn then.
Property or lack of it,
a man is on his way.
Is it a strange portion?

a new or old one?
nothing seems to fit it,
or take off from it.
A lengthening — a shortening —
only that synthesis —
whatever I have given it
to make its own again —
as mine.
I pushed it up,
and ate.
Hard enough to eat one's way
away from it,
but this must move across
and in.
The center as the heart,
and close to mine,
my heart subsumed in it.
Ingestion.
        Ask
the words of fools —
as I am — greater —
greater than I know to be,
or feel as done.
The neuter of such feelings,
where we rise against them
-small and portioned-
taken into myself.
Small sense — oh that —
sensing.
Pick it up again.
(and is the picking taking?)

Then a return to what could be addendum —
grim cut as earlier:
"All — all of it."
It is that faintness given outline.
come in from journey.
Rest.
     Easy.
All to all
       (as *in*
the other way of it.)
And there are certain spaces —

places cut off
                    rough.
Wherein the man in us
is doomed by what he takes
(and I have taken it
                         surely,
as any other man.
"There is a wound
straight through us"
edges open to a void beyond.
We may not plumb it all —
nor may we quite avoid it.
Holiness or darkness
other words for it —
the implements have rusted long ago.
No innocence — no innocence.
At the end we pull ourselves
beyond it —
                    travelling a space
in silence
                    where the dust is —
where the shades.
A place now, where the clouds may thin,
a winter sun,
                    late afternoon and south
above us.
Perhaps it is the way
in or around —
where we may go
through permutation of such light,
and touch the tragedy —
the instrument of wound
that none may lose
nor fall from.
Oh, it is the way of circles,
cry you no more innocence.
The ground itself has bled.

Suspense has had it —
nothing more than this,
that we may suspend
                         it.
Time enough to circle —

494

steadying on course —
the veer of hawk's wing —
flowing on a tail wind —
far over water,
or the tide of land.

How,
        portions rising
out of the sea
an importunity.
Take, on the face of it,
new land —
                again, the privy seal,
which covers,
                beneath a mailed fist,
the theft.
Such, as on islands, brewing,
thought,
        a very darkness.
How much — how much —
and did it (will it) pay?
That simple asking,
no simple answer —
countinghouse and ticker tape —
nothing so simple as the theft.
Rapine and slaughter.
Take, in giving,
very like it all again.

Until we reach a house,
                a heritage,
that shell we drag on with us —
Privacy?
        Ha.
It is shattered by the movement
of a breath.
And comfort is no word for it.
Other spaces —
                always those which open.
Break the shell,
                as if the yolk or kernel
lay there —
withered in its darkness.

Take it - take in -
and share whatever —
care and credence —
care —
        the very air.


## CXV

Lonely,
        as on a mountain.
left there
        -the cutting edge-
in rocks — a sawtooth range of hills,
now beached above the tide.
Within that tide,
        where I have been,
lust opens gentle
        like a flower.
Petals wilt —
        the tilt of sun —
that which brings the seed.
At times I have to leave it
        higher
on the mountain,
        to cut illusions.
One never cuts them —
one, as I.
We are wrapped in them,
done up,
        raw pieces of meat
in a butcher's paper
-leaking a little-
our blood through illusions
and miscalculation.
We are not lonely —
        even that
is denied us, and it is hard
to creep into a hole
away from sounds.
and if I go into a place
        without paper

(where paper is needed)
what than?
                    My oversight?
Forget the paper.
                    See the sights.
Hear — if it is the wind's ear
hearing
            lonely on that mountain.
Hard not to remember,
                    but that is a shell
again.
        Not sight.
An over-sight — so seeing.
Let the paper
            rot as all good paper will.
I would not write it on some plastic —
force and process
                left on the desert
below a mountain — bright and tattered,
picking up a light it does not own.
Lifeless — sand-marked —
                    wind-pocked —
never lonely.
All of this business of the lone —
alone —
        whose business?
Oh, the chill of blood,
                        up here,
the desert wind again.
The spark of light, as traffic moves
across the roads.
                Mere roads —
Ask for a wider one —
                    jornada.
Or dried by certain terms.
It is not dead —
                nor I —
the cosmic substance
rolls down hill,
                in sand, in grit,
a gravel stopping at the boulder's edge.

Much is heaped — rocks left in cenotaph,

a cursory piling,

                     masonry we do not know,
and yet a loneliness
                  induces
knowing.

Child of the blood,
what child may I bring?
rising from the things
I claim to be my own?
From valleys
still
     high valleys —
well, it has been my own task
climbing —
          hardly a climb
up.
It is a brown country,
not a dark one —
tanned as leather —
where the blood may leak —
child's, or my own.
It is all a hard climb
up or down.
What difference can that make?
How would I listen?

Shaking the foil of the past —
Ha!
      The sparks were beaten out
long ago.
         Yet, no catches.

It was a long time catching —
whenever — oh what fastness.
Eyes that open on it, see
no loneliness.
It is a judgement
reached and left.
I had come in, and I had left,
but I had now known such smoke,
nor tears as I had thought to.
Only the mountains.
Only these!

A life to stay with them,
or congeners of theirs,
a world fulfilled.
Massing attack
                    to east or west,
and with such clouds
as waste in flames
each night —
the crossbars of the sun.
Then I will go out on these —
the fragile limits,
paving light from substance
on the earth —
                    within the earth.
A gentleness not reckoned —
all the dark to follow
is not night,
nor am I lone, or lonely,
nor am I lone, or lonely.

**Sunset —**
**Mesquite, New**
**Mexico 12/6/76**


### CXVI


A little for the soul
-only a little-
returns again.
'Winter begins,'
                    a strange one,
though they speak of it here,
who know the remains
in this place.

As if, for the first time,
a clock had started
of its own accord —
                    the ticking —
(is forward, or not forward,
is backing
            the eastern route
an entrance note.
We are, by the clock's rite,
older,
            all of us desperate,

499

showering off the smell of our oldness —
a bath of dust.
Not so easy, what in our ease
we mistook.
                    (The clock strikes
a difference
                    from that community
the hands demand.)

11/20/76    It is the time in a secret,
Indio, Calif.    a status of one to one,
and that shimmering
under the heavy desert mountains
at noon — the line of mountains
though it seems a weightless posture,
and only the air is heavy.

The majesterial
                    "we"
how it tightens and shrivels.
There is only the 'I'
                    the 'you'
('thou', if the language will hold it.)
'We' are the two of us.
Keep it at that.
I enter no battles except my own —
                                        and
those with trepidation.
It is easy to succumb —
                    so easy
to side first with one
side
        or another.
All are so reasonable —
all of them.
            But I ask them
to tell me —
            to hear what
I do not want to hear,
                    really,
and I am left, in the end,
helpless,
        alone on a sidehill,
facing the sea in the sunlight,

500

to climb, helpless,
                    up
and away —
                    a lone thing
stretching at tethers  —
to distance.
                    I am not —
and no one is,
                    truly alone.
But a question of meeting
is always a hard one —
that it is not mere confusion.
(A dyad — that 'we'
only for moments
to hold on,
                    loosens the root,
so that the mere thought
of battles, or sides,
thrust and parry,
is pointless.

In a time, away from you,
I am writing this *for* you,
in love and in trust,
a dread that the meeting
will not come about,
or that if it does,
there will be things to flatten it,
dull its splendor,
as the splendor of mountains
is flattened by heat,
by stale air at midday.
that we will slide off the edge —
a mirage.

Though there are surrogates,
none can achieve
what is actual
— this dyad —
unless it is you.
Not that they might not,
given a care and attention —
other concerns,

but that I am no longer willing
to cloud what is one
with a generality —
dispersal of strengths.
It is not wholly an argument
revealing a small concern.
(Look deep, but do not search
in the sense of a wounding.)
I have asked it of you
knowing that I may not
expect complete centering.
What we have called
dead center
speaks for itself.

Dull cast of the sky
in its afterglow —
haze once again,
and a warning.
Some things are abroad in that land
which obscure,
as one goes east, away from the sun.
It is hard to remember
another system —
other galaxy in time.
But all of them, real enough.
And there was one hour
between noon and darkness,
when the outlines were clear.
So I move to you,
as I hope you are moving to me —
the opposite finials.
A journey.


### CXVII

How you will mark,
by sign or season,
certain credence given
clear of light —
                    of darkness
mark the whole of it —

that march —
                and that insistence.
(And darkness of the afternoon
comes on —
             a suddenness.
A cenotaph —
             minaret —
yucca in the desert —
tree on the mountain.
Mark it.
We will not come back this route —
others may find
                  or stumble on it.
And of these stones — a trace —
blaze marks —
colors stolen from the sun.
Alas, this way, and that one.
Column and flute
eroded in the wind.
What you will find here —
a way of nature
in its first disturbance.
Move across it
                gently,
that it may not break
or fall from you —
your feet in void.

The mists of the night
still present and gathered,
accured in darkness —
that the sun, by certain strength,
may strain,
                and finally remove it.
The mists of what I hear
or read,
       the same,
a covering,
until I bring to bear,
and find it not my own . .
Ah!
     mark you.
Mark myself.

The sense of journey —
raise a sense
of going.
it is hard work
generally speaking of it.
Do not speak.
The sense is lighter.
Yet we cannot keep from speaking
-none of us-
caught in words.
And sense of wording.
It is often as the clouds
caught in the mountains —

**Showers in the
Organs 12/17/76**

a mantle of them
in those valleys
halfway to the peaks
they give perspective,
and a sense of interior.
Words caught aright
are like that.

The daily brood,
the march pored over,
mark it well,

    again —

this opacity —

     clouds and words:

**George Oppen:
Route**

As George says:
"words cannot be wholly transparent"
though there is a luminosity
comes through them.,
as the sun through clouds.
Even on the darkest day
it is not as dark as midnight —
and another dark
being that place or time
when no one speaks.
Is it enough to observe
the movement of the lips?
Will that result in words —
an echo of language? —
only the breath of it?
I would scarcely think so.

504

Yet it is sometimes relief
from that tyranny —
autonymous to themselves —
which words exact.
It is folly to believe
our definitions all of what they do.
They rank as things,
as beasts at times,
that range the savage brush,
and our imagination.
Lexicons cannot hold them —
nothing can —
they are as demons
ravening our brains for flesh.
Beware the man, who,
in the wilderness
-his heart on fire-
succumbs to words.
He is a shaman,
and another breed.
And words are gentle
as a woman in her flux of love —
that comfort, also.
A mark to mark by —
and to come by.
Word!
          that strange thing,
no matter where —
how long outside.
They will not rot or rust.
Root in a place —
and pass on seed.
(Do not mistake the word
for its semblance —
echo, or any other form.
Not how it was used —
how it used itself —
repulses and attracts.
But it is that desert —
-mesa or ocean-
where it occurs.
Little we know about any of it —

until we go there —
little there
                    until
we come away again.
The marks are internal,
and they cannot be found
until the corpse is dismembered —
divine haruspex
who might find evidence —
putting it together
                              again.

The complaint:
that nothing gets done of a piece
— that it once did —
return to the words —
there is space there.
But the objects themselves?
Stone into sand
or crystal-that geode-
it will suffice.
It must.
yet there is no way
to insist on it —
the marks leak out —
glide like snakes —
and there is no end to them.
No end to words.
Will it suffice to say?
a posturing outside?
Set the dishes —
ceremonial bread and salt and rue.
All rites come to the same one,
all airs go round.
It is not so.
We are not lost.
If there is nothing to lose,
there cannot be,
yet it is hardly a thing to say,
or to place easily.

This started at a place in clouds,
somewhat within them —

though above the mass.
From it —
                the marks.
No holds.
Another time to think of them.
Some will be.
Some will not.
The marks as words?
Each one is blood.


### CXVIII

Sometimes to think:
If all this were in danger
-fire or flood-
what would I save first?
knowing that I could take out little?
(A shill or skirl —
                    birds in the smoke —
train passes through —
an aside,
            but something more.)
What would *I* do?
                    Anyone?
Leave it all — and walk out.
The flames behind give warmth —
an ash touches
                from it —
Achilles' heel or Siegfried's armpit.
(Brightening and strengthening
the sun through clouds, and
yet no sun.
                Is this an object?
How would I save the sun?)
And in the night, a sound,
that terror —
as some man's life burns out —
a holocaust, reduced
by dawn,
            to steam and smoke.
Some of us alert —

most will turn over
to sleep once more.

What would the salvage be?
what to count over
blowing fingers in the dawn —
perhaps something not counted —
seen last in childhood —
tossed on the dump by others,
unaware,
              if that last fire is death.

If you are in the desert,
burn desert woods
                    -only these-
drink bitter waters —
eat the fruit of thorns,
mourn these,
              if they are taken away.
They are enough to sustain.
All else is purged.
Sit at midday,
              under
the shade of rocks.
Well, go away, if it does not suit,
but take nothing with you,
bring nothing in.
It is the rule of the desert,
of all lands —
and there is nothing —
nothing open,
              nothing to give.
Fire on these mountains?
Clouds and wraiths of clouds.
Such sailors come
aloft the skies —
beyond them —
and the night flows bitter
in a lake of frost.
What it is —
and what its danger.
I go out into it —
lose myself that this be found.

In all this silence,
sound will open —
howl of the pack at sunrise.

There is no thing lost
that cannot find itself,
and will,
            again and again,
            from hollow to peak —
            that stance —
                        another form —
or what is found is lost,
And finders weep
at such a change —
there is no gain or loss
in it.
As ceaseless as the sea tide —
flux and wane
upon our parts —
                        our selves,
and such as what we bring
or call our own
We make so little of it —
what we have —
until the change compels us —
in despair —
                        to look at things
gone unfamiliar,
                        yet the same.

Ah, but in the time
taken to do the things
most needful for the self,
I rob another.
it is not enough to work
if such things happen.
I am alone, lost,
in the welter of these works.
Ipse! Ispese —
that the characters
become some smaller things.
And those things lose,
*I* lose —

only myself.
The lost one —
listening to the passage —
time — my own time —
payed out —
steel hawser and an anchor chain.
(It turns itself over,
now and again.
Do the slim books —
many of them —
make in size
        a larger.
I must ask these questions.
I must.
      Yet I must not.
And the one I rob
goes down in rage or tears
to sleep alone.
We cannot put ourselves
to escape.
A forward frowardness.

I think of it, and yet, I don't.
Fire or flood,
        or what will enter
blood or wine —
all this — and these.
Yet senses cry to them.
The morning rises —
          night on night.
The sun goes down —
its quietness, a voice.
I am alive,
     and you are.
Who are you?
Nothing is lost — and nothing more.
We go outside —
a few of us — to talk.
And in this place —
the lost things found —
(or were they ever
        things?)
No voice - no sorrow.

Nothing is the rede of it:
Its mete.

## CXIX

They brought me much I didn't know —
from which I could learn
but would not.
It all had to come from myself.
Some of it a pride,
not all.
But in that pride, born later,
lies a secret
that makes hard tissue,
wrists and fingers,
muscles for the journies
I have taken, and am taking,
for the most part
                              alone.
A journey away from those —
their voices.
I will not question them,
well meaning docents,
no matter what the sadness
at a blinded vision.
Those from the sheepfold
now are sheep.
Raven alone.

As a man walks,
                              so his feet —
taking to the contours
of the roads he knows,
those he does not,
where he may take delight —
sharp flints for others
unaccustomed.

The lay apprenticeship
-how one learns anything-
to go through these motions.
but when one is apprenticed,

he barely realizes —.
Wisdom *seems* to come,
fullblown.
Medusa from the head.
It is not the way,
and yet it seems the way.
We are spared some pains
if learning comes
in learning's time,
as any other time or thing.
*They* stand outside it,
seeking and straining to regulate
the heart's beat.
Those outside, stay away —
clear.

    (oh what would you do,
clear man?
How would you —?

                no,
It is bemused to ask that.
The unaccustomed feet
will always seek and look
to bridge.
There is no bridging.
Bring the feet back.

What each morning brings —
a rise —
to clear the head —
its passages.
May I not teach myself that much?
Long singleness of passage.
Oh,
    a man looks out in that.
(Darkness be over me,
and blind.
Darkness be damned.
I'll go out once more,
to prove the darkness:
What the darkness is.
What it is not.

Portion of moving

-wise portion-
what the teachers do not know
-would be-
the sweats of learning —
puffed, dead face of the student.
Not the hero —
                    in his stance —
and yet heroic.
Too often bitten,
I am moving on alone.
Take charge then —
helm and engine.
A far piece —
                    cry
horizon.
Rising from the sea,
or from the mist —
a levelling —
Believe it all —
not what is there.
High in that land,
to dig for stars.

What was it?
Did I know it —
did I —
            not — ?
Strain of remembering —
a climb —
and all one learns in climbing.
A way down,
all one learns in descent.
An interference
                    (descant)
And it is harmful
to know such things at the wrong times.
Clear the mind —
the air around it
                    remains clear.
It would hardly do
to take in more than ballast.
Loaded above the plimsolls,
the ship will founder

in dirty weather.

William Falconer

The helmsman's hands still glow —
he sees them in the dark,
but does not wonder at it.
The sea and air.
The mountain and the deep.
Do not clutter or affront.

Bearing the branches,
bearing them over.
Bringing the sacrifice —
dealing it nightly.
Bring the oil?
Well, that's old hat.
Somehow to know,
and somehow to think
of what I may not.
Know —
                    in emerging.
Use wisely.
Let me alone,
                    pundits.
I have a life to learn.


## CXX


And, if remembrance brings, or
brought the pain
we had in doing —
what? What then?
Sometimes it is not the act —
remains to be —
                    recall —
the savor of it.
What *will* act —
                    arouse —
is the kernel of the nut.
Then,
        *reaction.*
How it touches - me-
or into me,
                    or you

who sit the vigil with me.
More than act —
                    the waiting
through the nights, and
to the sunrise.
                    Chilled,
stiff before the remnants of a fire —
coals which burst in flame,
if wood and patience
come to bear.
(There is little moving.. —
desert lying to the fence
of mountains.
                    Shaft of sunlight —
first among the peaks.
A last adventure —
                    losing.

Recall. Full Flesh.

What did not happen —
brought in ways
that seem to be.
    Oh, blood remembrance —
remembering
                    blood
                         fall.
Each time I go in/to —
a place I have not been —
familiars crowd the margins.
I *was* here
-a part I do not know,
yet have acquaintance.
Darkness? Yes, and light.
Stretching,
                    walking to the end,
where the land falls off.
    Here, that I have learned
how much easier it is
to go handhold over hand
upwards.
                    Descent and memory
are precarious —

                          set on rocks
that move and slide,
and come down at the back.
Careful not to stir.
Beware, if that is wary,
do not fear.
These places — chimnies in the rocks —
one opening —
a flood of knowing —
what we may not know.
   Rise, rise out —
pure smoke.
Illusion or mirage —
careful on the downstroke,
feeling the way by staff,
cut from a native wood.

To the specifics,
what the story may be
-one of spirits-
look to that.
If spirits cast their shadows,
leave an echo,
                    by moonlight,
   fortune is gone.
If not, there is current,
will o' the wisp - hellfire -
bent to destroy.
Dreams are the casts —
these spells.
They do not cast them.
Ah, then.
            What then?
(Slight wind of the draw
from the valley.
Mountain?
             Turn to the rock face again.
Later, marvel at the climb —
extent of it to eagle's aerie.
It is no place to be,
unless one has remembering —
where others were —
ghosts and partisans:

Tension:
        Spring-in-the-box —
        struck warily.
        Take no season;
        care will out.

        Or that a young man
        looks to himself —
        attempts to avoid an old one —
        though the old one cries for help.
        Memory?
                  perhaps in memory
of old sadness —
the young man's blood remembers
and recoils.
A long way up and over
to the outside —
then will it in again.
The old man's stuck at his chores
stiffly.
Our pain — all of ours.
nothing — nothing new
                *under* the sun.
   Only the sun.

So much may seem easier —
— take for granted —
(its memory)
if only the fact grows smaller,
in distance;
or it may be reversed.
The sheer cliff,
           at first hand,
offers
      a few handholds.
Tufts of grass —
           a thorn or two
on the way up.
Often,
      it is loneliness
that brings memory —
focuses the sun's rays
through a hole in the rock,

drying the dust,
if the dust was once wet —
pointing a way.
                    Distilling a fortune.

(Travel light, if you travel
this way.
              Touch nothing
unknown.)

The cities lie below us —
a mist from the morning
-like memory-
surrounds them.
It will brighten at midday —
still,
        some blur at the edges,
something left over,
that time when it first lay,
immovable fact.
Slight change, slight rise,
world on world —
                        hinged —
cognate but separate.
Is it in memory
that power remains?
Coherence?
Microclimate into climate?
Hazzard such guess —
escape to preserve it —
only in this place
-all place-
              no severing.
Savor of such time,
and succor.
Assuages final thirst
and seek no word.
Nor is it all.
Sleep comes
              and no more foundering.
Stone raised on stone,
or stones cast down,
perform together.

I cannot say which ones —
that secret bourne
-passed on-
abroad,
                and in the dark.


## CXXI

Perpetual Easter —
                    the pasque flower —
La Passione.
                A color's staying,
heart'st blood —
                    blood red —
**Sangre de Cristo**  if that is not reflection —
1/20/77
                        afterglow for poppy —
flame to the leas —
last cup of wine.
As if the earth
                obeyed it
too —
        the fate
or bondage of the light
-enlightenment-
all of a piece
that it might stem from anywhere.
and make connection.
(Words — words again —
nor let, nor stay to them —
nor will they end
in simple meaning —
their wildness harking back
    to making in the sun,
a primal clay
or taking lustre.
Let it all spin out —
in credible!
                this is place enough.
Belief begins here.
                    Box *that* compass!

Spirit of rising

                    without the rise.
          Attempt to complete —
          but where would one — ?
          goes out to / becomes perpetual
          -not perfect —
          oil flows to the lamp
          before the lamp is empty —
          current through wire.
          Pulse/elipse
          of the blood.
          Finding some *thing* alive
          touches, merely,
          the life had always.
          It comes surely as a voice,
          a vision in a word,
          then flickers and lowers,
          brightness again,
          takes over at a place,
          flare
                low,
          and rises.
          Merely a suggestion.
          And what suggests
          is truth of the matter —
          not the facts.
          (Seems as if it moved
                              quick
          -probably doesn't —
          never an illusion, though,
          find out the meetings;
          by the long gate.
          Smoke, or is it mist?
          Fire and water,
          balancing (complaint)
          Complete it.

          It was a dark climbing
          over a winding stairs
          in the rocks.
          It seemed as if it had been
          placed for climbing
          -purposeful-
          but other purpose must have

touched it.
It is not a use,
but *put* to use.
And if those mountains
-rocks on fire-
ice catching in the fire,
pasque flower bearing fire
where the earth renews-
all seasons poised
upon the verge
of all again.
In this, we open up,
perpetual planting —
harvest by the side of it,
and not a contrast —
more than what we knew
in either one.

But how can I —?
-only myself-
be judge of this?
There is no judgement —
no one left to find a way —
or synchronize such time.
Perpetual — yah!
Misjudged again.
We're on the edge of it,
and yet have nothing.
Ritual!
        and that's the making.
        but in ritual of death or living
        nothing comes from plan
        or forethought,
        and wise men, in their care,
        care most for nothing. —
        what is most palpable,
        yet shuns the light of doing.
        A fine day of it —
        — sun through mist — the early morning —
        burns away by noon.
        The shape is clear again.
        Give us this rest —

as that which holds:
The snow on peaks
a summer's day.
The heat below
in winter morning.
Laudate —
(laudate)


## CXXII

In . Con .. Contra ...
(dance)
in
contra
dance.
In dance —
*in*dance .
So spaced
the spaces.
A hesitance
redeems it
not or
sub - ex -
other than —
come joyous.
Come and dance.
Wisdom as a lack of wisdom
opening.
Ideas - inception -
re-
ceptor.
Solution as a way —
avoidance
of the problem —
and to solve is
not to touch it.
Leave the answer,
and return - oh
dance the problem.
*That* is dancing.
That is wisdom.

Make the problem - window
in.
Or drop it, all,
water
     drops
        pen
          dant.

Clad in grieves —
another age —
or these —
        such presence.
  Any age
        -the dance-
They sit it out.
Bring in a light —
Perform in darkness —
that the feeling makes an age of it.
Compression - steel -
a spring.
That all of it is in the sound,
and colors sound.
Refuse me not this little spot —
a place to rest —
the sward around it green,
or snow in winter
-high enough-
it clings - on spaces where the wind

**Los Organos 2/2/77**    is least, and north —
*that* space,
        the folds
in dances.
Not that it should be
the province of a quicker life.
As dead men's bones
the rock face —
        scar — oh touch the land.
Premise on a minor fault.
Place on the place that fell away.

Symbols, pointers, as the sun
through rock hole

strikes the lode.
The rock has faulted,
and the sun goes free.
The lode remains.
Disturb it not. Grant still the spot.
Water
       falls
            de
                pendant.
Ply of the wondering.
(What you speak to.)
Speak as dust:
                a going through —
drops
      pen
          dant.
Water which displaces,
leaving space,
              proclaim it
dance.
As an enginery —
this cunning.
Place as portion.
Lot becomes the spot.
Break into motion —
break it out —
the static flow.
How else impinge these
things in disjoint?
The flow of dancing
makes large moving.
Tensed
         touch of
quietness
            disturbed.
(If timing helps
                it
moves the joints
or
   rather
moves
      a stiffness

out of them —
                an oil
or balm.
            In answer
go.)

A flurrying —
bring passage yet again.
The top of it
a straitened case.
In all particulars —
then, set them down.
Intensely skilled —
pretend the dance.
In rage forewarned,
I break again.
                        (*I* had not entered it.)
Slow as the movement —
let it be.
It must remain
the dance at best.
Perchance it is.
and let it be.

So on the premise,
mirror fault.
And let a man in mourning
feel the weight of graveclothes
moving —
penants in the wind —
fluttering as feathers —
feathers as the wing
let by —
            a flying dance.
Correct it by the compass —
needle set in such a fluid, the
pole is accurate,
and yet moves, dancing.
Is that dance a laughter?
Who comes by it?
    Why would any man?
Come
        by it?

Only for the dance,
a laugher, is it?
dance — sub, and extra,
where it will reverse
     revere it.
Play on the words —
as tones — a mastery —
and let us in.
Water
          drop and
                         fall
dependent
                    pock and pinch..
Then, let us in.
It is a way outside.
It is a sense outside.
It is an inward thing.
It is the shearing off —
old bolts to let the engine free.
All this in dancing —
this in moving —
this in cerement
or ash or snow —
the field of it.
They compass, who are dancers,
   feel the cloth from altars,
node from branch,
and find these problems,
worth and weight.
Solve none of them.
What passes —
bend of any —
iron flesh - a mystery -
be joy or sorrow
in this dance.
Let ligament arise and
hold the earth once more.
It would be known —
the freeing of it.
Sense, break sense in these,
as egg yolk in a bowl.
It tempts us all —

outside a measure —
struck.
      One sound only.
Tense it then —
we're into space.
Complain that load
and board upon.
Water
    drops
        pen
           dant.


## CXXIII

Adjacent to the dream —
'a ring! A ring!'
Or from it.
No tide, nor let.
No stay to turn the wind.
'A ring! A ring!'
A sound and echo
from the rigging of the night —
these branches tossed —
'A ring! A ring!'
(As drowsing in the day.
A quietness.
        The hum of bees.)
Then what is gathered?
Which is dream?
Adjacent —
        as the stems
-cones upward-
from burned trunks —
a spine or snag —
the charcoal gleaming in the sun
wherever fires went.
Let and stay, wherever —
ring, and ringing.
Sound within the ear.
It is the pulse tuned.
Hearing is an inside thing;

outside, the toss is sense
                          less.
Let them know
              how to.

Then for the dream,
a place —
and in the place
the quality of dream —
its ash and fossil —
what the names come by,
or what they give.
Some sound of it,
and as the ring is sound —
the sand birds —
                    (sound birds)
Break it off.
Little said of it —
                    well said.

I climbed a little hill
with ghosts
-their wind-
                around me.
Deeds, but what are deeds
for this?
What sense of them?
I have gone down —
a way into them —
but I am out, and not immersed.
It was a day —
                fanatic —
tempered, as the sun was,
with an edge of steel.
I tried to keep away.
I had no business there,
yet drawn on to the pit,
the ground dragged open —
left to bleed.
There was a scent of it —
a sense
        decreed
in it.

**Las Palomas, Chih.**
**2/19/77**

528

Sound of birds.
It *is* the morning.
Wrestle with the day —
and yet,
         no portion.
I come into this:
vague restlessness.
I do not know
         what.
'A ring! A ring!'
A solid fire —
magic to the morning,
                yet
drawn in an ordinary dust.
What it will blunt or sharpen.
Stays itself.
I am carried out,
foot, or head first —
nothing more than that.
The striving:
Nail scratches on a wall —
weathered in the first wind —
none to follow.
But the small sense stays —
the flowers —
              petals in the wind
that break and scatter.
It must be another time.
Oh, the sense of words
is waterlogged.
Simple.
        Nothing is.
The edge of fear,
and nothing left to fear.
I could see the mountains
plain from any window,
but I was nowhere near them —
left to try it out — alone.
A dark depression
Weights were lifted,
but I felt them pressing —
a version of it —

something grasped among variant texts.

In the shell, the taste is bitter.
leave it to ripen.
Coming from the wind,
return to it.
The day began in sun
and clouded later.
Feint of this dream, and
climb away from it.
The days seem surer
in their past.


### CXXIV

How, among shadows,
those which are not,
or hold a shape
beyond a dark enclosure,
reach no evidence,
in this silence —
sounding.
                    (Is it blood?
pulse sounding in the ears?
enclosed again?)
Above them,
                    I may stand
alone, on the shape of it,
a small peak
                    among greater.
Uptilt — a record of other times.
In this one,
                    shadow —
those great shadows
placed across,
held down in stone.
It was no climb here,
yet gives that sense —
a tensing space —
the very blue above us.
And always we look to any cloud
for shelter.

Pyramid Peak
2/21/77

530

Would that *they* would —
could compare us.
a darkness —
or the very blood might spill
for thirst of ground.
(Stain first, then pulse of stone.)

This kind of a shape —
the shadow palpable as dust.
Do you know figures?
Can you see them
against the mountains?
the very mountains sharpened
in the passage of the wind?
Its rite or right —
divine it.
Hardly living, here to there,
its compass.
What lies behind it?
Is there purer air —
that, too, a shadow?
Many times the sensing of it,
now upon us.
Bear upon the memory.
Stand, ears lowered,
weather the storm.
I've come up here,
perverse as any wind —
its shadow.
All my shape is shaded
under the rush of it.
Shapes — well there are shapes
enough to give men rest
in darkness —
when the wind dies —
restless and unwilling —
to a shadow of itself.
It bides and waits to rise.
(The commonness of fear,
each puff and veer,
the underlying outlines
of the old laid bare again,
and scored —

                    a limit
vanishing once more —
the high moonrise,
beyond which, nothing is.
The map falls off.
And hence,
                    good fortune
for tomorrow?
It was yesterday.
What makes it?
peak on peak —
withdrawn in shade,
obscured, but actual.
A compassing — all points.
Could we arouse it?
Animus?
                    or in the sound
of wind rasp
lose the blood pour?

It is a healthy morning,
only the morning,
we within it, filled
with poisons —
those distilled from night.
Tense storms which darken
the better days emmeshed
in them.
Can we hear such things
and still deny them?
Comfort of the womb —
a fiction — there are no wombs,
no windings. Wind
has pulled us straight and taut.
Inched over, upward.
Hunched, a standing to the storm,
a lee edge nowhere.
We are pariahs,
always on the outside —
shadows.
                    ( am still
above them,
standing at the best angle,

holding to the rock face,
claiming wind.
Shout down:
'There?'
Are you still there?
The torrents of the sea,
and torrents of the land —
a heaving back.
Can I wander farther?
Break me these sticks,
as fire tosses into dark.
Go out on a fist,
as well as any way —
all ways must go.

Whereas,
                    but there will be none —
no proclamation.
A man tries —
is at the easiest way —
and there seems no other.
If there are memories
shore them up,
living, actual, deeds.
No repetition.
The only way in to such
is dream, and portion
of dream
                    — approximate —
keep at them.
All are mentioned.
All - All.
Husband the memory
as a thirst,
and let it be no more or less.
Sink into fortune —
fortunes *will* be told.
A short way above this place,
but in the mind's eye,
no longer way or place.
I am coming slowly there.
Memory beyond its congeners.

## CXXV

from Aguirre Spring

There is nothing to remember —
so I remember it —
not memorable.
(Unmemorable? Immemorable?
Some word to fix the state.)
One tree poised along the ridge,
and there are many others —
larger trees — bent or tilted
to stand out —

        this one, squat,
        well-shaped — well enough
        for this distance below it.
        Nothing to fix or hold —
        so it fixes.
        I wrestle with no image —
        the tree — actual — pine
        in its proper zone.
        It is winter there,
        more winter than below.
        Some snow. Fixed,
        it is a memory.
        It can be reworked,
        numbers of times —
        in differing directions.
        Because I have seen it —
        *my* pine —

                *my* tree —
have a care, you birds or squirrels
how you treat *my* tree.
And have a care of this —
my memory of it.
Shortly, and ago, I woke up to that.

Is it not good
to take a look
at ordinary days or things,
for qualities of both —
though forms of them are changed —
the elements?
Void is nothing,
I may not fill it with pronouncement —

534

stick with the tree.
So hard a passage in,
oh, break me on the rack of it,
stood up,
a single tree along the ridge.
And in the night —
my miseries compounded.
What are there?
no shapes,
and nothing palpable.
When I believed the day,
I could believe its morning.
Standing at once place
                    lower,
was I not in place?
surely aligned with tree
or point?
So large a shadow
fingering
needling me —
but a security
locked in to it.

I would believe, then,
-belief for place —
that I would return to it.
Not the same place or tree —
that changes, too.
Animus is left —
and in the wind's eye, only.
Bits of it remain.
That lost projection from the mind —
what *one* thinks —
another's silence,
concerned merely
with a list of groceries —
few things *are* more apocalyptic.

And memory is cursed —
a bitter water in the well
runs salt.
Among the streams of it
a man is lost —

the maze webs over him,
and he cannot sort out
what best will serve him —
a detritus —
.boards and stones
under the smothering of it,
as if they were rooted,
only, in dry rot.
The man smothers, too, —
only his embers keep warm
there — a little while
                    longer.
There is a hard wind
blowing through
                    and around him,
stirring the fires —
cooling the ash.
he leaves — a dry skin —
case of a caddis worm —
worn, but not outworn.
Let in again.
                    I, too.
Thinking too much of the ridge —
its ordinary tree.
Leave off.

              Hold it in journals.
Let it rest,
and let the mind go dark.
But there is no room for that,
and the fingers tire.
It is vanitas,
but is it such
the preacher talked of?

Complete the day in wrath,
let it be this day,
or any other —
only, let it
              be ordinary.
It does no good
to sleep alone and think
of things removed and quiet.
All shadow —

all.
The focus of those few
who stand with faces
cut and bruised,
eyes smarting —
throats thick — uncleared.
It is a time to be abroad
(or stay indoors)
no settling at the threshold –
half a way as much another
way.
Whisper . Finger . Length .
We've done it all,
and what we're facing
hears no sound,
and sees no vision
in the vision of itself.
There is a balance —
there are keys and forms —
but none where we might
look for them.
Merciless — ah mercy —
pity and the rest of them.
Complete the pattern
as design.
We held our way here —
may we not come back?
There is no backing.
Half a piece
-alive there-
well, who knows?
As well to ask, 'Who goes?'
as this, or know a blinding.
Pulsing, the motion,
tensing the dark.

And what are tests for shadows?
These, from many places?
Days on days.
They strike a rightness —
stride and bell it.
Silence in the night,
or wind,

          the winds back
to another place.
The thought of silence, over.
And the blood drips
from the wounds caught back.
Laid bare —
once more — once more —
an echolalia.
Thence, take it.
(How that inversion came
and cased it —
stepped inside.
I wonder,
          but the step
of wonder clears.
So little time for it.

In flood, or season
out of flood,
the river courses bite
the marrow of this land.
There is no creature
able in it.
Mistaken sense
come closer.
We are bitten,
and the teeth are shadows.


### CXXVI

Four pathways to the wind —
four feet to hold a man
(though he may stand on two of them)
What is it the seasons cannot do?
Or will a rule of four turn three?
Three legs to level easily
-a stool-
          a triangle, the strongest shape
in engineering?
                    Four
takes more time —
                    a patience

and a craft.
                    In seasons, then,
that patience.
Nor will we name them, wisely.
These pathways do not hold a name —
are reached alone,
and by themselves.
Whatever that wisdom
-not to name-
the rest of it in boxes
sealed in their naming,
let them be, or not be.
(Cedar, in a long season,
gives its scent.
Stay close to it,
but know it only in the sense.
Whatever I'm at —
you, or other,
reverence for it,
three, or four, paths —
or balances.
Do not, quite, disturb it.
And there will be one
in any move
which cannot take the name
or space between —
whatever else might be a likeness.

Stars — stars — the very stars,
go out, or come a nova,
ready, then, to die.
Four pathways —
three times four:
twelve gates to one —
the city — polis —
or the land which suffers it.

A long time talking round
becomes around,
only to return a pole —
one subject
                    and the paths.
We cannot simplify what is

-already-
            simple.
The great wheel holds.
                        IT cannot
break/gear.
(Seems so in scarce knowing.
Let it not be seen in part.

Compass of the wind let by —
a rising storm or levelling —
could be another will.
*Mine* vanishes — this place.
Sensuous time — heat of it —
the pathways clear and close.

Length of days will not account —
nor length inside.
Preform, and predicate —
a business lessened/leaning —
path —
            one must open
on the other side —
or does — or not.
Hard to stride here —
authority will not bide.
Mention - it
                  slides past.

I saw —
as in a dream, I saw it,
three columns rising to the sun,
of dust or mist —
its composition secondary
to what I saw —
those paths, or legs, that hold
and binds us.
It is a secondary wish —
that two should make the systems —
what we hold/
that which holds us.
Length of days will not
suit it —
the instant captured —
lost never/forever.

Anapra, New Mexico,
3/1/77

Ways of getting in —
the back ways to a back country.
And when I am at a loss
I have this.
Whatever is a whole
performs itself out of loss —
out of things forgotten:
oscura/escondido.
Now I'm putting in and passing,
counted by myself,
less time and pathway.
I am nothing, and the dust subsides.
Well, they've taken me,
and taken me along
to such places —
scanted —
        forgotten —
the place in the book is lost,
although the reading goes on,
and must go on.
It is the moving eye —
the lips in motion.
Tempt me —
sensorious — each time
I must return to it
from pathways —
symptoms clamoring to be heard.
These idylls — all of them —
the ones in torment most —
have caught me up.
And I am on a way outside —
there is no living here.
Four pathways, yes
and twelve, and three —
the none of them
           as one.


## CXXVII


Guilt and gild —
weregild —

     weird —
the say of it.
A conscience.
Pure mist as gold.
I capture it, and so do you.
Some source brings wealth —
and wealth is gilded —
guilt - uneasy.
Nothing rests.
The landscape changes —
changes me,
a place where I am lost at first,
then make connection
with the others —
what is past —
and buried to the hilt — to root.
(The root is possible —
the day has credited
the possibility.

If such a time were rain or sun-
-but all that comes in wind and
sand sharpened.
The clouds hang in the mountains,
rooted there against the wind.
A guilt of stops.
How do we spent ourselves?
The trial pends,
a speaking through a law —
an arbitrary speaking.
Guilt afterwards.
There is none, now.
What little do I pick up
from the earth?
A news of blood —
were violence
         no guilt.
A stranger might pick up —
There are no strangers
here or anywhere.
The rooting is no easy matter —
nor a feat —
yet all judged, rightly,

is at root.

Clearing! Clearing!'
That the sun in strength
comes once again.
A warmth in clouds
                    (from clouds)
the swaddling broken,
sharpening the peaks —
an afternoon in warmth.
A lazy sound, or wind,
against edged clarity
It comes again.
It leaves us.
Clearing! Clearing!
The songs outlast us —
grateful in the light.
And sing again.
                    The chant:
Clearing! Clearing!
A root at clearing —
sure and strong.
The guilt has faded
in the heat,
against the rock,
the rising tide.
(Yet clings -its darkness
brooding in a shadow
far from sunlight —
where the sun will reach,
at best, no longer
than an hour —
dark and cold again.
The best days turn to lees —
are brackish.
How well to remember it?
Memory is forgetfullness
gone wrong,
sour as milk in thunder,
and that is guilt again.
Wisdom! Ha!
That's a tooth — no more.
Mixture of the strains —

they blend the colors —
black or white —
all the same — the same in guilt.
Break me in showers —
sparks or heats of other sorts.
It will be —
                will be able.
Time for the trial
-the usual assizes-
nothing is so usual —
nothing brings or loses.
Guilt!
            And let the guilt be spoken of,
and known.
*My* guilt —
                and if it all is known
and judged
there is forgiveness,
even in the reticence — the sentence.
It is waiting on the edge of conscience
kills the heart,
and hangs the spirit
in the wind to dry.

We must use the locale,
but not as if we owned it
-tenantry — a stewardship —
is all the love of land.
Yet there is guilt
that seeps in blood
that others have not dealt us —
the ancestors —
                    ancestral shame.
There is no way out,
as dust in climbing, swirls,
obscures the sun.
And many times a man walks out
to shake his fist,
or spit in rage —
that fragile tenantry.
The land is old, and
we are old in holding
what is spite.

This rage — a silent fury
in the land.
There is no weregild large enough.
A payment. No,
we do not make up for it.
A simple footprint lasts and lasts.
So, what if in the morning
I wake up
-the birds already laughing-
and I cannot reach beyond the sheets?
I am cursed
for what my blood has done,
and I must share
the trial's opening.
"The fault of our time."
The fault of any.
Nor is it simply conscience,
blame or shame of it,
there is a way in or out,
but no man knows it.

(Under the poles,
upon the field,
a place for testing.
Fallow ground. Fear.
And some will die —.


### CXXVIII

*He spoke of it exactly —*
*meaning to exact a prize*
*from fault and opening —*
*the death of fortune —*
*devil's brew — a reason.*
*And it was simple — all he saw —*
*or heard. No Magic in it.*
       **********

One by one,
          they do not come
whatever season.
They mix, incongruous,

the days themselves no map:
From morning clarity
to storm by evening,
or at noon a lull.
Who tries to find a pattern
loses what he has —

            his own.
It once was easier,
so the old men say,
but I may say the same,
including what I've known
by time or some convenience
other than the spot I stand on.
(Way down the cliff, through sheer,
looks easy from a height,
and features mingle in a blur.
We are not recognized —
pass through without a word.
a hard composure —
pressed rock.
And of the rock?
some record —
ferns and snails —
other times lie flattened
to a glance —
under or over the sea —
they seem a regularity.

Then, in the morning,
rising to another day —
washed clean from sand
or wind —
'the dust has settled'
(but it is not safe
to make approximations:
The day with caution.
In morning,

           such and such —
a splintering,
and the care comes
fully rinsed.)
Hands move at approximates.
A man is chilled,

not by the night so much
as these assays
to name again.
All night I've wished,
now, what comes next?
an inner climate
broken down to weather —
what is usual —
a morning bowl of soup.

Next this:
A day the dust settles
                    out
of the mountains
into the earth again —
a freeform hardening
or sculptured —
                    caves a grain deeper.
Is it hard to be?
or for those caves:
Gates of jasper, or of horn.
Why such?
Jasper, on the road.
Or horn, let be.
A necklace of seed
-light and dry-
tosses incessantly —
picks whatever breeze there is.
The dust has settled.
Mountain stands, a grateful heap
of stone —
            to sun
or is a light sent grateful?
Can I be?
Away from it, I think I am.
The composition highlights,
and the wind, with clouds,
flies over.

Stone, stone,
a wizened face
upon the ground —
the sun will light you.

Pass the light
to earth below
this resting place,
and catch, catch
echo from the moon.

Or as the sun on dust
laid emptily
along the way —
the catching light —
it will not do
unless the magic
opens into it.
Sharp road, first locust
in spring wind
                  (the sound)
take time enough,
and be such brothers
stone
        alone.
From such small things
these others rise —
small in their kind,
to make whatever
lies in seed —
true to a disposition
we may not dispose.
Heterae —
why that to mind?
Companions on a way
that is darkened —
better so.
What a man knows,
he will, in some sense,
regret, before he is done with it.
Mixtures — oh — those desires
come and fall away
as easily as undercut.
The banks fall
unerring to the flow of water.
Night mists —
those, even in dry country,

exactitude —
or what is asked as price.

Each morning, every,
what is told?
conductus —
                    capped,
the transplants in an alien soil.
Still, the heterae —.

*Stiff, in the wind —*
*hardly to account for it —*
*these grasses hug the land.*
*Ghost of a mountain —*
*ghost of a range of mountains —*
*dust in their snow —*
*a restless shift.*
*Ghosts of the dead —*
*Spirits of the land —*
*Drop through the wind.*

**Sierra Blanca**
**Tularosa 3/13/77**

As we went due north from Tularosa, toward
Carizozo (the town whose name means nothing in
Spanish or English or Indian, unless it signifies crazy)
we came through a loose dust plain — reddish sand —
which ascended in clouds from the west — a fresh
wind carrying it. In places, the high peaks around
Sierra Blanca were nearly obscured by it, only the
outline of the snowfields shining through — ghost
mountains — ghost power. It is well to walk gently in
such places. The spirit power is vengeful if it is treated
with disrespect.

As the dark continues
to hide the clouds
which hung on day
-a smothering-
heat - its bounds are
undefined.
I rise again —
no stars.
A Jewish exile
-if there is one-

harder than Jewish exile —
dark of the night
(the morning cleared.)

   And Leasburg: At the river, on the fishing paths,
through a tamarix copse — early spring — and the new
shoots equivalent to larch. One thinks of Siberia in
June.
He says these things:
*"I never knew heaven*
*could be terrible as hell*
*or be as bright."*

**Jerome Rothenberg:**

**Jerome Rothenberg:**
   **The Notebooks**

*"exiled —*
*and driven mad."*

*Terrible things to say —*
*a glowing ingot in the gut.*
*A place to go away from,*
*but there is no going.*
*Oh birds of gold,*
*of burning feathers,*
*take me from this place.*

If there are doubts in failure,
enough in anger to keep me on —
this for all of us — no more
is needed-
          scarab and magic
work it
       deviously.
Commence in all of this
to move the ways.
(A character of landscape
is its thirst.)
Requiring a way,
             we find it —
sharp stones a proper spur.
Employ the wit;
it steels a claw.
Time will apportion —
time has —
already seeming.
Confused?
        No —

take the exile —
the evidence of heaven.
Make madness from it.
Madness will rivet home.
Praise madness.
Guard fury.
We have need of it —
and take an ordinary step.


## CXXIX

The ins and outs:
-entrada - salida-
crystals of the telling —
in the —
how a man is raised,
and at the moment falls,
debased.
Tecolote — little owl —
(water in the wind
depresses —
                outsides
are ins —
compact of hope.
A shape in such.
Yet more than shape
arises from them.
I will come, and I will go —
at once the progress,
and the threat rehearsed.
Of such a day such comes,
and more expects to come.
Luck, but luck as fortune
is no blindness.
Talk of the fates,
the parcae —
old women in their shawls
prepared to give,
not blind.
Bent to their voices,
chorus: in and out.

What of the crystals?
what will *they* form?
What fall of dust preceded them?
(The land, turned west,
is east again.
habit becomes necessitous —
there is no praise or blame,
nothing done —
                    no loss.
The curve resists
                    and holds.
I'd pitch it all away
if things came clearer,
yet the sense is anything
but clear
                until the snub
of in or out.
Whom could we call
or place in line???
What business has it here —
(but that old marble,
hardness, which is clarity —
a water after mud has settled —
will not, and cannot
                        vanish.
If we have lost it,
it will not lose us.
The beginning of a day
-and many days-
                    hence.
So come the bright beginnings —
later, tokens.
I've not known it —
easily escaped.
Just now, another context —
3/20/77     how the robin sings —
dry country for his wetness.
Place the sound,
another compassing.
Run it through.
That it may be
-might breathe

552

without nostalgia —
essence being.
All essences alive —
strict days, and looser.
The timing was —
that I was out at being —
being in, no closer.
I had neither.
I was around —
but that is distant,
beyond periphery.
One for confidence,
I lived in self.
I say it of another
from a footstep,
leaving bed, determined,
in the step, an angriness,
no nonsense.
Still, a compassing.
Can we sense so much?
or would the answer be
incomprehension?
Clouds move, and we do,
(habit as necessitous.)
Well spent,
or was it life we left
to mean a thing?
It is not the property
of things, when things
resolve themselves —
ideas and likenesses.
Put it as:
This wash,
that stone.
As marker in the sea,
a barrenness of fact.
*When* I go out —
the spirit, in.
Collection has it —
congeries of fate —
but not the words grown
little/big.

A charm arises in the air —
and that is closest —
*not* approximation.

Thrown from his horse
the rider walks and follows,
on a branch, a scrap of hide,
of hair — a broken bridle.
he is not confused by it,
must settle in again —
entrada/salida.
                **********

On such a windy afternoon
as this one
(warm —
                spring wind is
often warm,
though has no reason)
I delight in little things —
the wood I carried
from the mesa
-just enough for evening —
and the table where I sit,
also of wood.
The restless clatter
of a chime outside,
a voice or laugh
next door, and borne away
before I hear it
clearly.
Such an afternoon.
Such wind.
                **********

So give this day —
and give it up
to what it brings —
there is no greater way —
the ways are devious
as the writing of them —
large or smaller —
generous becomes the niggard.
All that I spend,

and that is spent upon me,
rich and heavy as the heartwood
bleaching.
Come, come again,
and take the day in dying day.
The sun tomorrow
enter out and in.


## CXXX

It shall be marked upon —
-this page-
its virgin stain
runs down the blank of it.
That such an object
is the bound of what contains it —
no more or less than that.
A fustian compasses.
The days remind me
of themselves —
in being gone,
or still unthought of.
A temporary slip —
the chronicle becomes account.
What was observed (as seen)
was not observed (as kept)
a date, or some such marking
on a calendar of saints.
Nor take into consideration
the *fact* of anything.
It is all too loose,
its tightness, pat.
& set dying
to the wind —
Hilda Morley    a deliberate misreading
for my own purposes,
blown.
As, at the ditch bank
this afternoon
(kinder and gentler to say
acequia,

acequia madre)
I sat and looked at
ordinary brown water —
something sleek that bobbed through
the sluice gate in the dam,
an otter?

**East Side Canal,
(acequia) 3/21/77**

Probably a piece of wood —
ordinary,
perhaps.
- There are no ordinals.
I sat, back up to the sun,
and filled a space
as ordinary as paper.
And then,
after that,
the misreading —
deliberate, even malicious.
Put it all together,
but it will not touch
that which is virgin,
if there is such.

Into one or another
there are many pockets —
many things to balance
out.
Yet I put them off.
It is hardly worth the thinking.
Doing comes as something other.
New morning, and the depth of it.
Only the eyes remain in shadow,
dark with blood,
behind a vision.
Clouded, it will rain
across that vision
-staining it —
removing it.
(Another section, white.
Keep on.

I want something small
out of myself,
to answer for what

I do not know,
and do not have,
can never be —
that this small talisman
will make sure
these things —
                out,
and out of myself.
Misery of that —
(a flat planing, admitted,
*might* take a bit further.
Flat places are not
always,
                black.
Put it down, and let it stand.
There is a lone wind,
sounding late at night,
around the chimnies of the living.
There are no days
to think of anything but days themselves.
It moves around them
(wind)
but days must wear within.
They are not last or lost —
figured in transparencies —
yet they must hold up
in what they are.
(Put it down. Let be.
A puff of smoke,
or is it dizziness?
Left from the sleeping
done in places
left.
Avoidance of the things
that must be done?
The time is shortened,
spurred on the peaks
of what it cannot be.

Retract the claws.
Self-beatings are no purpose,
and they cannot know

the things they really are.
Almost time to close the doors,
go on, and if another door,
it is another.
Nothing to go back to.
Whatever found, take on.
A staff lies to the hand,
always in the place
where such is needed.
The cry of loss
comes only from the lost itself.
    Inept, a man remains so.
Whose wisdom? Compassing?
Approach the end and know
there is none.
Aphorisms — packed,
like lunch — a necessary baggage —
at times too much of it.
The wheel and the column —
all that will rise.
They come this way —
then that —
remain all of a piece.
There can be no hesitance —
yet we are hesitant.
We break the charm —
but do not,
                as we cannot.
There is nothing to reform.
All breath is a reforming.
The page lies deep in wondering
-ciphers across it —
yet nothing changes.
in the midst of danger,
a good night's sleep.
Good night.
            (good night)
Tomorrow, such another.

# CXXXI

Like a cathedral
(concept of one)
it stands unfinished.
There is no finish.
it is not the ritual
that left the scaffolding
behind the nave,
to blacken, and let the wind blow through.
"And I went up into the mountains.
I was glad to be there —
glad of them,
               and of myself.
I was alone, and not alone,
companion of wind on the left,
of snow on the right —
the last wet snow of the winter —
an eternal wheeling and whirling
-so it seemed to me —
while across the plains
and many miles to the south and west,
I could see a place,
perhaps where the wind came from,
bright, and in sun.
It was a vision,
and the dimness of the cliffs
where I stood
was another vision.
in sequence of clouds
which have snow and water
in their mists.
If I had known how,
I would have prayed;
but I did not, and let my standing
be whatever prayer could be."

Rock, in its split,
the unfinished outline —
a cathedral in scaffolding
up to the break of the sky,
and the sunlight.
A shaft in the thirst of the land.

**Los Organos,
across to the
lava cliffs of
San Miguel,
3/27/77**

559

After many days
the water has dried,
   and the wind, still keening,
rises in dust.
That we ride with it,
anonymous,
let there be no doubt.
It is easier than going there
to find identity.
The angles and corners counted —
all remains so
-held-
            unfinished work.
Ways over the mountain?
Those, and back again —
all counted —
cease nowhere,
nor begin.
A violence in knowing —
when or where.
Thin flake of sun —
off the curl of island waves,
one time, and at the bottom,
silent and suspended,
easily the same.
Voices of the ritual
wear through the stones —
a masonry is not forever.
Preclude it —
perilous stop —
the talus so loose
it came away in my hands,
yet may have lain there
for centuries
before I disturbed it.
Into such things —
completed in such places —
touches of the living
-no less —
            more real
than meaning.
(Something raised to stick it.)

(I was talking one day,
to place another.
No different either day —
they all commend to one
which is not light nor dark,
nor has a single place
beyond us all.
Let none be loose
in such a handling.

The track —
old burns, and such as live —
charred stumps
half buried in detritus —
leavings of *our* sorrow.
Give no emotion to the wind.
Remembering, it all comes clear —
a clarity.
Voices mention it —
they do
              pass through.
Link of the land
to others linked.
Joined, not in clusters,
nor by chain.
They speak it — all of it —
commencing/quitting.
It is almost the voice of the workman:
'Half hour and hash time
soon gone to hell.'
The track is not pitiless,
no pity known to it.
Nor anger, silent
in a brooding wave —
itself - itself -
and surety the rise.

The wind without the dust —
the wind, as on a deck at sea —
good, and beautiful — the wind:
with dust/without.
A vigil in the wind.
It watches.

**Acequia Madre,**
**Mesquite, N.M.**
**3/29/77**

561

Never fear that watch.

Talking to myself:
And on the road I met a man:
Ramon.
'Hi, Ray.'
             Χαιρή
*That* was easy —
coming/going —
a freshness in the breath.


Come long ways, or by short —
it rises —
how it comes:
the ghost of many feelings,
be it strange or simple.
Eyes that turn to wind
turn down in water,
what they make, themselves.
So carefully the *man* at rising,
all the rest in motion,
of a movement,
nothing to be thought.
Let it be a circle of light
we do not know —
beyond the simple fires
to others — simple in themselves —
but further off.
A current in the wind there,
which lies along the skin
in ways we do not have it here.
And yet it is the same
-a part of it-
and built upon the scaffolding
beyond the last tower —
the last stones heaped,
but not yet fitted.

A blaze. A blaze well spent,
and by the torch
of a reflection.
Coming, we will find it warm.
Days for sacrifice,

**Ramon Vasquez,
Mesquite, 3/29/77**

562

and yet no offering —
laughter mingled
-this of gods, and that profane-
All of it allowed,
and gathered in.
In some great way,
the death of conscience
-that there is no need-
a worship with no fears
out and around the way.
And this cathedral
        centered.


## CXXXII

Numb to leave it,
at the moment, numb
but thawing.
Return is not the answer,
but return is
what it is, an actual.
(As the water rises,
                washes,
on the side of the abuttment,
graffiti vanishes.
Dissolved, it flows its message
to the sea.)
Sliced open, entrails show,
and dry, and darken
                -poor entrails-
cooled and dead before the body —
living on elixirs, echoes,
mirror images.
To descend a longer way,
no man will find the secret
at the heart.
The living center is dispersed.
It lies along the skin.
We do not have it in the center —
small pieces
        dumb and frozen —

eaten and assimilated after dark.
We are, as we are not —
entombed/interred,
yet only ask to rise
along the wind,
or blow as dust —
the body's bulk.
Numb, numb to leave it —
wood char and ash.

**Albert Pike:**
**A Journey to Xemes**

One man, his cry:
   "I have always been hustled about the world without
the privelege of choosing where I should go because
instantaneous circumstances have decided my move-
ments, and the consequences have been that I, being
the person most interested, have had the least option
in the matter."

What did he expect?
In loss of chance,
or such volition,
the chance is made —
is the most personal.
It bears that seal.

And burns as real —
the gold in ingots.
Buried and forgotten,
something holds it there.
It will not be found again
for any use —
returns its proper elements
to such as have them:
What the dwellers in the dark will keep —
no Fafnir's horde.
And come along this way —
the sound of those that do,
mixed with others.
Burn as real.

Las Acequias —
let there be veins to carry blood or water —
all the humors —

let them flow, and let them sound
by winds which are not wide:
the fevers.
Let them hold, and let them free,
as if the penstock opened.
Let the marrow grow.
Let them be for all
-from all —
let nothing know itself
except in all.
(Afternoon — the red of sun on clay
on dust
on damp
                -a workman's shirt-
the watered fields —
a business clinging to the nerves.

And then the fires
                        in their lightness
sprang away.
Once started,
nothing was that stopped them.
Turned and twisted,
chips on water
                    -like them-
vanished and come back.
Nothing stopped.
A hell against the bank —
the heat against the wind —
(And this, downstream;
it lies in state
as always —
such a movement.

I thought:
A man, most ungodly,
or godlike —
more, a troglodyte —
and his name was Theus.

If you will wonder
why one must chew
over and through these things
so many times —

it is partly the changes
of a landscape (perhaps)
or the shadows on a landscape —
what we see, and do not see,
finally, must convert
as we admit that we did not see it
whole,
                and still do not —
still make the mistakes.
(that ungodly man
who returned to his mine.
It is a day earlier,
as a day later —
and the bundles are fresh
to be classified
(we did that)
we do it again.
Ah, Mr. Theus.

If there is night wind stirring,
what of the day?
                        wind or light?
(It is a moment only —
passes around the eaves.)

So let us wear away —
an ember burn
this — rising —
ravening within the wood —
prepare it.
Nothing answers,
serves a purpose
where no purpose
                        is
swerves
        thin.
It is the rising
and uncertain name
of mimicry —
what moves and does not live —
a semblance of it —
a direction in the wind.
I find it —

nowhere.
And blow the petals
each from each —
he loves me —
                    loves me not.
There is, in numb desire,
a resting place.


### CXXXIII
### PENA BLANCA

Vanish, into the earth.
*You* will not vanish there,
unless you rose from it.
There is no source of comfort —
give it truth or lie.
As one man might, on rising,
say:
        "The trees.
The trees again.
The trees in leaf again,"
and say it gladly,
knowing that the leaves and trees
are of the earth
-that he is-
waiting for it —
no desires for more than earth.
    integer vitae —
who will not build a house
or city with another thought
than that of where
they came from,
must return.
That all things breathe —
as mountains,
and the forests on the mountains.
Land, and what walks land —
a pulse that lives in it.
But there are those
who live away from breath,
and count their learning other.

Here, men are hired —
raise their flocks for gain.
And they will die, not knowing,
never having looked.
They crowd themselves,
and laugh at vanishing.
For them, it comes as cruel.
No pity for them,
nor any blindness.

You will not vanish there?
And yet you must.

And at the top of the mountain,
beyond the trail:

**Tortugas Mountain**
**4/4/77**

a shrine, with broken glass
and candles —
a stained madonna:
'Rogad por nostros.'
Nothing matters,
and the shards will vanish, too,
into some earth.

A campfire lit, and used,
tended a little while
from smoke to coal,
and then abandoned —
keeping to itself —
still hot.
Whoever lit it, sleeps;
but on the land
the winking eye of fire
glows and pulses,
fitful in the wind.
Or, steady to the stars,
a shaft of power
open
        navel of the earth,
its cord a heat that touches
upward.
Silence there.
A place of power.

But in the remnants,

ashes, potsherds,
tools, whatever,
is no power.
It returned from them,
and found the earth at once.
A glowing, and a rising,
point on point.
It stays with earth,
and none may borrow it,
who will not give it back.
It is not found by greed,
or avarice.
It will not lend in usury.
All those who come
to reconstruct a history,
do it at their peril.
There is nothing in it,
yet the power stays,
outlasts the shaping winds,
or rain,
or if the earth itself is spit —
remains and flows,
transfers whatever touches
and believes it.
There is no further rise —
nothing visible
to hold a shrine.

Dead bones —
the bones are living yet.
The wood, in tracery,
skeletal, is brittle,
but it can bring forth
in a certain season.
Come and see it —
do not lose that portion
which has breath.
A scattering of flour
-first libation-
given that the earth may eat and drink,
but also, that the one who gives
may link himself once more.
Do not attempt to lose this place,

or find another
poised above the core.
The center, everywhere,
-one center-
and one place to find it.

First the wind,
and then a funnel in the wind.
A rising spout
that touched the wind
and touched them.
It is bad luck, they say,
-an evil thing-
to cross the path of such a wind,
or feel its breath.

Prayer is a long vigil,
and without words —
without an asking.
It must come from fire.
Return to it.
It cannot come to one
who asks as favor.
Power wilts.
The root is loosened.
And the flower dies —
bleached with the chaff,
crumpled in the eye of the storm.
But that is only what the seeker finds
and loses.
Power is, and prayer, within the power
of the earth,
and as the earth may hold it.
Motion to the past
-beyond it-
come and find —
the high place - open -
always open.
Those who came,
and those who will.
They did not make it sacred.
They recognized.

**June, 1976 — April, 1977**
**finished at Mesquite, New Mexico**

# Book V

# The Commentaries

*for George Quasha*

The Interlocutor:
I don't know how to enter this. It is all too neat — and
as if I willed the finish — almost as if *this* finished it.
It cannot be what it is.

Should I look at
or along the object?
Both. But what beginning?
At surfaces, weight or size
in being;
along the sources,
and that other which refuses —
cannot end.
Ask the man at midnight,
talking with his angels.
As a history, he found it long,
along.
Ask an/other his/story.

The Interlocutor:

It carries weight — is seen neither at nor along. The
philosophers who claimed virtue in either one were
blind to flow.

Then from a place I visited,
these words of a desire:

**Rumi**    AREZUST:
The QAL and HAL —
tension and outpouring
flow/along.
(or that harness
which a workman sets to winch:
a come/along.
QAL and HAL.

The Interlocutor:
Which shall be the first of these? *What* tensions?
*What* flow? Commentary? Make the comment.

From the elders —
their own speech.

At times that serves,
or blurs, to polish
later.
        Give this credence:
As you can see,

**Peña Blanca**    the mountain itself is a small one,
beside the mass of greater,
but has a strength they do not.
Even the miniscule
-a photograph-
places it.
The house, as the mountain,
should sink into its ground
enough to root.
But it is all so fragile —
nothing stays
except a source
-good or evil-
cloaca is cornucopia.
Shit befouls a love.
How dare we intrude
what is not real?
What *is* not — ?

        The Interlocutor:
        It all begs a question, with a doubt. What is not, is,
        indeed, real enough seen at a certain angle — that it
        makes a thing — and a certain shape.

The quiet night — ha!
few enough to experience,
may lead into doubt
or worse,
            on burning ladders
down.
A man lives his life
rung by rung —
sometimes a quiet niche.
He calls for that sweet death,
but it is not bidden —
only in its own time.
There could be something further —
set off —

set around — not fenced.
Well, in the taking,
more than fancy.

Worry at the bone of it —
bone worry,
teeth to shake it.
A man thinks. *I* think.
Stilling of conscience —
there will be none
until the end of it.
I cannot judge what I cannot know.
First of the way to come down.
Yet each hour has its moments —
lights and shades into bitterness.
The bitter days —.

    The Interlocutor:
    It comes to one realization: That what we label
    impulse or spontaneity may be just that at its inception,
    but it is very rare that it ends as it began. It
    reverberates, and the consequences are profound —
    often hideous — and a destructive power persists. I
    am not advocating caution to the point of inhibition,
    merely that we must prepare ourselves. What we
    call reality, is, in fact, simply one more fantasy.

Maelstrom —
as any other whirlpool —
a Norse word,
until you're caught.
It becomes immediate significance —
the only true signature.
How does one rise, or die?
One more sense there.
The shadow, stronger than its image,
is the actual —
   comes from source —
may be the true beginning.
What we take for objects
are not as solid
as they appear.
It may be, the actual persists
in an abstraction

(to our senses)
is no abstraction at all —
these hills and rocks
the true abstract —
a place where we attempt
description —
agree on recognition —
recognizing nothing.

    The Interlocutor:
    I accept it all. In acceptance, I reject. I move along the
    curve of space.

The heat of the flower
outflushes the sun.
Another heat — more pitiless.

At this point
what suffices?
Where does one break off?
the voice, merely an echo?
(What voice
            and in that voice)
Who is to say,
"He doesn't mean it?
isn't right?
or what his meaning?
He *is* right.
         He knows?
His rights are his —
no others.
We are not constant in our shapings —
the making courts illusion,
if that mirage is either
dream or one reality
poised upon the other —
what has surfaced —
no pure thing.
We cannot spare ourselves.
We do not —
         helix of the sun —
the shadow does as well
or more.
Standing in wet boots —

the woods around me,
soaking - soaking.
And the net of the flowers.
Seeds - burst.

> The Interlocutor:
> Poetry and philosophy are irreconcilable, since they
> both attempt to occupy the same space. Art is the
> more humane, and sometimes would like to make an
> allowance, but that is impossible. Poetry often sounds
> *like* philosophy, but the reverse is rarely so. Art
> springs from intuition to its incarnation. Philosophy
> hems and haws in the corner.

What is made as work
falls short.
       The joy must rise,
pure, of itself,
          to darken later
in our atmosphere,
It is the tensing,
not a teaching.
Take care of it.
Take care of me.
So little stays.
in taking, talk of it.
In sense, a sizing.
Darkness, and we come whole in it.
The breaks are actual.
It is a high place —
turning there, to works
remaining
       whole.

> The Interlocutor:
> I function as an introduction — at least I think I do.
> Thus far, there has been nothing save full tide —.

Not the wisdom of silence —
that has not been given.
Even in the deepest despair,
the work goes on —
no way to escape it —
nor will a man leave himself

in his furthest projections.
An overlap —
the way things function
at a moment —
yet do not fill a void —
ache and thirst.
Moving forward — but that is nothing —
nothing *is* one or another direction.
Nor is it aimless —
some things connect —
coherence at a chance
is nothing more than chance.
Ask me no more questions.
I must not hear to answer.
I propose none of my own —
let myself out
               a door —
another opens
                  beyond me.
Make no mistakes?
Hold here onto worm rot.

What we know or learn, we find
in our own amoral time,
but what we learn does not
depend upon it —
                    reaching out
beyond time's history
-no matter where-
to things which do not change,
and snub men short
against their boundaries,
The old saws cut,
and dogs worry at the bones
so worn as not to tell
their lineage.
We move along,
                are tempted,
and fall by.
We do not know what faded
until another season blooms
from our bloom's meld.
In this, a settling.

Stir the lees in.
All of it is drink.

No matter what the tempting,
much holds
on little holding —
hand over hand —
let down to the bottom —
series of echoes
chambered in the heart,
valve and stem of it —
at that place,
                    systole/diastole
let go again.
Whatever form it takes,
it is not void,
except as void takes its own shape.

> The Interlocutor:
> Whoever attempts to put this succinctly, runs the risk of
> labyrinth — a maze, from which neither he, nor anyone
> else whom he attempts to involve in such a system can
> return. It is not law, nor is it cruel.

At times, trust to mirage.
To have thought to drink,
may not bring drink,
but it will rise in its stead,
to fortify,
                    beyond the thought.
A presence deepens.
If it is illusion,
then illusion is actual.
A breath exhales,
congeals in cold like smoke —
and leaves a residue —
a film on glass, on wood.
Then:
        "*He* was here."
Or some such —
benign/malignant.
Whatever past is past,
and cannot be.
Some sense it easily.

Others pass through.
They never know,
                        and wonder
at the fears of those
who feel the dread
of what lies heavy from the past.
A sure, inexorable thread.
One must not listen
                        overlong
to voices in the corridors.
They are real enough,
bearing presence.
It is not good to feed on them,
or to desire such company.
Other things to take —
and let them vanish —
burst in sunlight.
        The Interlocutor:
        I am diminished by my necessity. It is not loss of
        will — my own — but I retreat through it.


Texts or variants —
written from and out of a man's pleasure,
as pleasure turns:

And on the fourth night
rain came harder than ever.
It was no storm,
but stagnant.
                It wasted us,
and beat the whitening stems
of new leaves
-dissolved the buds-
there were no roses.
In keeping with our inner rot,
it spread from out
inside us.
                We knew no shelter.
Bowed and trembling,
                        darkened
before the sun went down —
a sun we never saw.

It was that season,
following that presence.
To be elsewhere —
                    where?
It merely rained.

      The Interlocutor:
      Chorus, as there is always a chorus, even if it is a
      voice from off the caves.

Ludens:
We play with love and death —
destroying the bitter and the realease.
Folly and peril.
Unfortunate and numb.
We do not go on easily —
jolt and shock.
Age brings no wisdom —
merely talk and regret.
Ludens.
And yet there is little of it
on the grim page.
Work will not
-can not-
joy is a free bird.
We see and sense poorly,
little that is there —
each man a difference.
Nothing brings understanding.
The leaves cast shade
in varying degrees.

As words recast,
they tend to lose their force.
The arbiter is not the fashion.
Nothing made requires
an explanation not itself.
It has rained six days.
I need not say it.
The rain continues.
My voice does not.

      The Interlocutor:
      This becomes difficult for me. On one level it robs

me of my force — my being. On another it strengthens
me that I become a thing in myself — that my words
are required — not as words, but as a being — that
this should be the form and sum of my being.

The dark pages:
Things die out too late,
long after their replacement —
yet their dying, in their day of death,
takes revenge.
Long after opening a chest or closet,
odor hangs and permeates —
a clutch at the heart
if nothing more than that —
opening old issues
to what can never die.
The eldest things remain
-the best of them-
and do not die.
The others suffer in their shadow.

What is a fiction?
Am I here?
I do not answer in Cartesian,
nor could he have known.
Try as we will,
with our small breath and flare
to open,
we may remain the best and highest
fiction.
Nor, dwelling further,
do we go in bournes or coffins
to a place we think.
What we know is scattered —
ask on wind — in water —
flow away.
We cannot take our spark
from what loses fire
to its source —
can't remake it in itself.
I have asked a blessing;
that does not ensure it.
Only I must bless myself.

Take flight from this —
there is no fiction in the void
fired round us.
Space commands it —
interstellar in the real.
Is the real.

> The Interlocutor:
> At the very moment that we know enough to know
> that we know nothing, the need to make pronounce-
> ment becomes a necessity. A two-edged sword. There
> are things to be said: A tiny residual pollen that
> may grow in another motif. The rest, no matter
> what its seeming 'wisdom', is foolhardy — an un-
> necessary burden.

Whatever is shaped, comes out —
each reach makes it now.
There is no older place
which stands free of change.
Returning to its constant,
we find no history.
Qua patres difficilime adepti sunt relite turpiter relinquere.
Do not despise the old
for their age —
nor for what may seem infirmity.
There is much to learn there,
nearly as much as
we must turn away from
Gloomy and dark,
                       yet
Bells sound.
There is a way through,
if none up or over.
(But not to break the head,
nor stiffen.)
Will we, ever,
understand the human wedding?
or the human
in all the monstrous things
we attempt —
and where we fail!
That at one time, even the inhuman

gathers to itself, and is.
Presumes a human shape.
It is no morning,
if we are not in the morning.
It is no thing
sings in the void,
yet is, again,
against the wall.

Make me the play of myself.
I am no further
than I have been, at play.
*I* am not constant,
opening the circuit —
make or break.
That says it
                    once.

          The Interlocutor:
          Take me in context. I am the left hand from which
          my right was made.

"Make it new."
That terrible indictment.
It comes close to it,
then vanishes —
                    nothing new —
no slate to wipe clean.
The very mention clouds
-but not the air-
a level land in other land,
blackened.
"Make it new?"
Make it.
'It' and 'make'
inseparable companions.
The manifest
is made.
AFAEEL A AROUZI,

The feeler — his feelings.
There is the song.
*I* can have no more —
nor you

The Malpais,
Carizozo, N.M.

584

-who lay beside me last night-
the same this morning,
yet not the same.
We are changed — not new.

And then it broke.
We came open,
clean and naked in the light.
All we could promise:
'To love, and go on,
wherever, in whatever days,
whatever change.
The wounds — cleansed —
dripped blood — no poisons.
We rose over the edge
of the world —
a wall there,
but behind us.
There was no other way —
nowhere came through,
no way to wonder at.
We cannot go that way,
now/never.
Whatever done,
retreat belies it.

    The Interlocutor:
    Looking. Looking easily at the different hands.

Such motions come —
the *length* of time
moves outward.
It is a sense and not a measure.

**William Bradford's
List of Greek and
Roman authors who met
unlikely and strange
deaths: A tribute to
their paganism!**

One who died —
'his brains dashed out
by the fall of a tortois,
which an eagle dropped
upon his bald pate.'
Another —
'torne in peeces
by doggs
as he went home
in the night.'

'drowned as he was swimming
and washing himself.'
Or last:
'had got great store of money
by his playes;
and lost it all,
by merchandise,
and was inforced to grind
in a mill.'
And on such evidence,
the prejudice of creed
strengthens itself.
A generation of bigots
begetting likeness.
Not to forget:
"Qua patres dificillime/
    adopti sunt nelite turpiter/
        relinquere."
Reverberates.
Shatters a wilderness.
When the fathers have no credence,
the strength of the sons withers.
They are no longer able
to raise the rock,
nor find the sword and sandals
secreted beneath.

> The Interlocutor:
> The tide's ebb may hold longer than we know — a
> slackening — loosing of elements. it will return to
> flood — clear the heat from rocks — put its world to
> sleep.

Salt's essential —
an aether —.

> The Interlocutor:
> Anything in use becomes beautiful through that
> use. That, only. All men recognize that beauty, and
> some of them attempt to copy it as an artifact. A fatal
> mistake. The stone wall is dead, unless it clears
> fields and defines them. it proves only that the work
> that a man does and esteems, extends — an aura
> from him. No one else may make use of any part of
> it.

To justify —
set in a line
with other lines —
that difficult distance
brought close —
foreshortened once again —
yet, is it
        -ever-
justified?
Cutting to the actual:
What a man wants
is what he needs.
From it, he draws substance,
goes to that blend
of acid and sugar
which makes his life.
Respect it,
though the taste may pall or burn.
It is only that the man desires
                        truly

what is his —
grows into it
               clean rooted.
Regret will come
from that which he has not taken,
or passed by.
Justify it there —
a supple line.
How much is needed?
need.
Want is only want.
To justify contracts or spreads —
either expansion.

Cruel, but authentic,
days, and days' rain —
how it suffers the earth,
and the earth suffers
with, and out of it.
Presage and after.
Thinking of a day:
what does one do with it?

It will do nothing
for or against.
A pre - stasis.

    The Interlocutor:
    But where do the words cut through verbiage? As
    much as a man wants is in the words, but the words
    allowed their own growth. They go elsewhere.

Stretching a column,
or over a column
Broken — an eggshell, say,
blue as the light,
blue as itself —
no color.
Tense and flexion —
It may not break here.
Thence, clouded.
    The Interlocutor:
    —is a virtue.
    Catch it if you can.
    It's seldom in a woman,
    and never in a man.

    Horizon's bending —
    horizon
        tal —
  Hora -
    Ahura Mazda.

The Interlocutor:
But, you see, even in the legends, we who are
transplants revere the stories from the lands of our
ancestors' origins, but we are driven by the new soil
to those of the primal people in this land. Alien in
both places, it is difficult to make amends.

What the wind has carried
away from us
        is still real —
trailings — high water —
the leaves are beaten —
wilted in flood —
        their flux.
A puff of smoke
      -hard-pressed-

hangs.

    The Interlocutor:
    I do not think there is anyone other than myself who
    should live the life that I do. Myself is limited.

I wish the real world
were as real
as I make it out.
It can be interpreted
as self-pity —
some of which
-and including the worst of it-
I cannot deny.
But is it wrong
                to
-once in awhile-
ask for a sunset/mine/
or that she who is the beloved
lies in this bed,
my arms?
           herself and myself
mingled
          to the point of sleep?
That which is in me
               pumps/pours
and moistens
          (pouring)
that which is hers.
We have not lost ourselves
in losing that
            precious identity,
and we do rise up, in love
                again.
To lie down in love.
             To rise.
Ah, real, real world — .
Your thighs —
          your thews —
your good works
          parting.
You - my love -
        I am
your love.

                    I am not
wanting
            now.
The talk
            diminishes
my love -
                in simple and single terms.
As:
      let me
come!


            2.


Thing of itself —
spelled out —
old man — his young love —
yearning —
                that yearning.
In that place
do not torture me
with solace.
The heart does all.
The hand is powerless
                            without it.
It cannot begin.
He who does right
without the inception —
blood-beat as his center —
does evil.
He cannot atone in work,
unless that work is love.
The gift.
It cannot be said that things
come right without the spirit.
No age, in its thought,
can transcend it.
Nor is it good to force the locks.
Love is itself,
                    and nothing more.
Stays, only of itself.
The old man to the earth,

the young earth in its age,
as age comes with the birth.

> The Interlocutor:
> As a man grows older his interests take the shape of a
> melodic line. It may not be the line that others follow,
> but it has a cohesiveness which was not so important
> to him in his youth.

The connections:
How the old and the young
meet —
          walking to meet —.
It is not personal.
What does a man create from that?
It depends upon where he is going —
who travels with him.
Few do,
          Yet *they* do —
all of them.
thing of itself
spelled out —
the solace at the sting.
Scorpion
          upon the land.
Tension breaking.
It would be 'in the way'
as that is two things:
along/an obstacle.
Creates itself anew —
a new thing.

> The Interlocutor:
> To see the beauty in a rain — incessant as it may have
> been — a waterfall.

All small things
without preciosity —
small only in the way
in which a size
hinges on another size —
physical, and nothing more.
This is the setting.

591

What goes into it
depends upon a choice —
'what you make of it'
Make well.
All of it is worth the effort —
the struggle to come outside,
or go further.
There is mention in wind —
the softest —

        susurrus
(that takes leaves at night)
one thing after another —
all held in coherence.
A mead, a reed —
inch or ell

        mere name,
some measure.
Take measure beyond itself.
It does no harm to feel
quietly
        among the low things
around us.
In reverence,
the great liturgy:
There is something deeper than the sound —
where the sound goes.
No one has been there.
No one knows.
Something deeper than sorrow
where the sorrow goes.
No one has been there.
No one knows.
Deeper than pain and flesh
where the flesh and bone go.
We shall go there soon.
No one knows.

Dart of a fly —
        flash-dart —
quicker than fly.
Quickness of venom —
sting of the wasp —
quick and dead.

The Interlocutor:
Bury only that which is dead, not that which is unfit
simply because of its present state, but that which is
new — the present —unfit to stay above ground.


Do not force —
the ground is fallow.
Crust quickens in rain —
dries again.
No stone is curst.
(the greatest gift denied a man —
his solitude.
To grow —
that 'grateful shade'.

    The Interlocutor:
    Because a man's intuitive processes may have outrun
    his actual proof (Q.E.D.) and he may have, in certain
    cases, falsified experiments to furnish that proof, merely
    to convince those who are looking away from something
    which could be intrinsically important to them — is it a
    wise thing to discount his contribution out of hand?
    Doing precisely this, and perversely doing it each day,
    have men achieved *anything?*


Drawing from wounds,
we suck there.
Poisons left —
the arrow plucked again.
Good talk — but left
as talk —
       the closeness grants
a solitude.
Fresh rising —
color of the skin suffused —
a sunlight
carried from itself.
I do not know the day
more clearly for it.
A vast, and breaking sound.

New day! New day!
Io! That we may move,

encompass.
Not knowing, will not change it.
The hawk still circling,
sky still blue,
                    powdered,
in full heat.
(If I had not known — or known.
There is nothing left —
the dust of hindsight —
many things gone away in it —
obscured —
                    changed as the colors —
sky - another.
Little enough to go on —
a floundering.

(A scattering — the wind —
the wind that lies along,
alone.
The open end of fate —
no vortex —
simple as a breath.

    The Interlocutor:
    What is it that I think each day, seriously? There is
    much that I think *is* serious, but that is of another
    fashioning, hardly a thing that I can trust. I see fire
    making and breaking around me, and then I see other
    things. The fire is made of the simplest things, but
    that is not enough to say that is always simple. Nor is
    much of it of serious import — barely enough to root
    and stay alive.

Nebulous as sound:
these concepts —
though the sound is finite
in its own bounds,
and the concepts may be
elsewhere —
placed in a balance —
acted out.

A tracery — this walk away —
it leaves account

that may not rise again,
but carries a potential —
threat, as if the cloud
hung stagnant,
                    waiting.
Narrowing, the day becomes
an eye, squinted along sights,
and some are taken there
one after another,
                    sped
and ricocheted
into the darkness.

What seemed opaque,
seems clean —
seems clear —
and both are seeming —
nothing moves against
or for us.
We do not.
The real is fantasy —
let go —
            let be —
and all prepare —
It seems a sound —
a singing —
honed for sharpness,
sweet to cut —
a ritual poured out —
its words in patterns —
hardly known —
but rising.
                    We obey
in trance.
The circumstance,
some altering of it —
no, it is all the same —
try to get back —
But where is no place:
A loss or two —
                    a man or two.
Far inland, looking
for the kelp rocks

rising out of ride.

Until the world
                is world again,
I cannot teach,
              nor any man.
Your world is not my own,
nor should it be.
             Thread is broken —
trails the wind —
and there,
           trying to catch it,
ravelled out.
Not all my friends are visible.
One
     against another
may be.
        Objects and spaces
are all spaces/objects.
Viewed so,
the abstract and impalpable
does (do) not exist —
coterminous and determined.
They are small enough
to slip by —
          screenings —
cause for nothing.
Despair and alarm
do not apply.

And such a world proves easy,
if we think it so:
We have only to ask
for what most pleases us.
We beat on doors
we close ourselves
-slammed shut-
It is this place —
            the place of danger.
We ask these questions
which are none:
In this place
-such a world-

is there any poem left
to write?
or any man
-walking the ruins-
left to write it?
There is —
he answers something left
outside himself.

     The Interlocutor:
     It fluctuates. Sometimes, in anger, or frustration,
     sometimes enough fire left to kindle and destroy the
     rotten wood.

Whisper by this small stream —
and trail its waters
-falling over
          piecing-
to renew the thread.

     The Interlocutor:
     Ritual *use* is not the ritual itself, and in many cases it
     is the antithesis of it. If men were aware of this much,
     many of the cruellest mistakes could be avoided.
     Hegel was right: There is an unwholesome nostalgia
     in the recounting of history. Those who do not learn
     from it *are* doomed to repeat it. but repetition — the
     repetition of the ritual form. If that is exact each time,
     with no growth, then the ritual itself dies. We must
     add, and at the same time take away.

Before the day begins
            -fairly
for the others —
I must be up and about it.
Their morrow greetings come
as I am about to fall asleep
-a whole day passed
in doing-
what is better done
in silence,
        lone,
even if it is lonely.

The day spreads evenly
in twilight,
if the clouds are still
drawn around it.
Before the day begins,
there is no other beginning.

Doom shut —
all that we say
is doom.
          Forever doomed,
whether said — or not.
The choice is put
—not easily.
Whatever a man says — —
Cut the trance!
It is almost a time —
not time, and all time.
We sit out our indecisions
sucking thumbs.
Never a way to look outside,
unless we are out
                    and in.
The watchword is 'around'.
Beyond,
          and in
the doom.
Door open to the door —
no one else.
Where it is put together
depends upon nothing.
Fee simple is the doom.
Attempt to get off the page
is off the living.
The attempt is there,
                    always,
but there is nothing more.
Puff of smoke —
                    another fate.
The moving goes on.

    The Interlocutor:
    I blow on my thumbs when they chill. I stay away

from that possibility as much as I may.

A problem in history
leaves the history behind —
the only historical motion
                                   possible.

          The Interlocutor:
          What one says breaks up into the type of saying that is
          in the words — not by force of the sayer. This is the
          way across, and it is the difference between communi-
          cation and magic.
One ear opened outside.
What places and concerns
must be subject
to the world around it.
A lesson for masters.
It is nothing that hurts elsewhere.
There are those who say of war,
that it is holy;
that if a man would feel compassion,
he must find it in a way,
and nowhere else.
The twisted faces of the dead
bear evidence,
and where one goes beyond
says nothing more of it.
In this dark cruelty lies
the true ambivalence.
I cannot say more
than what I say myself
-turning another way-
renouncing more than battles
in that turn.
It is hard to make a way
across another way.
Some find it possible.
The rest of them go by
and scarcely recognize
the older way.:
The sound of wind and sand,
or water —

what will move away from history
to what was prior.
Remembering is no small thing —
what to keep —
what to lose.
Faint odor —

             past blood —
past roses.

Put out the flames —
there are no more.

Omen of hawk or crow
-take it as omen-
-surely-
but not an omen good or evil
by its heritage.
The history lies full of blunders
carried by the letter,
not the ritual
in what it means.
As there are rituals for tribes,
for men alone
within those tribes —
a hard clean face.
We are about to go,
almost to begin again.
Slowly and slightly
carry the stiffness
to a place it frees.
There is another knowledge.
Fresh fire is new fire.
Legs are old and
need that cleansing.

    The Interlocutor:
    What I have said most, I have not said at all — a saying
    in the impertinence I carry — simply my being on the
    page. I cannot carry this in any other way.

The reach along the way —
as if a man put in his hand
by the door,
and found something moved for him —

a place —
shelter from the weather.
He would live here
in hard seasons —
go foraging in the spring and fall.
It was a doing,
but undone in the attempt.
No men here.
*That* man!
        (pack on his back)
at a crossroads.
Looking back,
          no man at all.
It is the fear of falling
keeps feet to the rock.
Lean in, to the cliff,
away from falling scree.
Tense for the doing,
he will go back.
He is other than I am,
other than the man on the road.

No joyous bird flies willing
into darkness —
nor full into the light.
It is suffusion.
Suffered, rises
          out.

Strident,
      to stride —
he who strides —
shadowed —
         leaf shade —
his back in sunlight —
ranges — — —.

Not in a theory —
all theory crushes in the hand —
specie - specific -
what it brings.
Be, in the bringing,
wind or less.
Begun from gnomic form

to the opening,
a final clearing.
Motion makes
motion made.
Sequestered.
Cup of tea or coffee,
early against the sun.
Sun rising with the stream —
bouquet of flowers.
Such as
            is.

—each drop a crystal.
It is our fate
to move objects
from those places,
(even if they are places
owned and structured
by such objects)
where we do not want them,
to others
            where we do.
(Brave try.)
We must not forget the objects
in the moving,
yet to take the movement
as objective —
in itself, and
for itself.
The objects are not lost,
nor energy —
that highest object

        The Interlocutor:
        Statement of form may be the form. Often is/is.

If I bend into this,
I come up with very little
that I did not have
erect,
        but that little
makes a constant differing
movement —
                ratio

to what moves —
wheels in sunlight:
The milling.
Days of many duties
create solution —
the more or less —
less as all —
be all.
Do I?, or can I?, rise to this?
I talk it through,
find little in the talking.

> The Interlocutor:
> How often it is that we cannot reproduce what we
> understand — language or some other act, perhaps
> through another discipline. It forces into and out of
> consciousness — all of it the result (but not a cause) of
> conscience. Let it be thought of in these terms — others
> — but these must come first.

Reaching into that section —
the heavens (the earth)
all the same.
We come out whole
without trying.
It is never the same
with effort.
Stream comes down
against rock —
                    resistant.
But the resistance
moves upward.
The water courses,
seems to expand —
cups over.
There is that much,
and only that much.
Being one day in it,
we are all days —
that much sweat
off the ends of the fingers.
Do not stand firm.

Stand pliant,
and the flow of time
his/story
        moves around you.
All the lessons spent,
only to be unlearned,
if we will know anything.
And yet fog hangs,
obscures in ignorance.
Another way leads through it.

    The Interlocutor:
    It is good that a man, by turns, applauds himself, and
    recognizes his unique genius (how can he give from it
    to others, if he does not recognize what it is for
    himself?) and repudiates himself in another breath,
    and thereby knows himself as nothing. It is *not* good if
    those two elements are not securely welded to each
    other. A faceless man is left, if he does not look into
    his mirror, and often, for both aspects.

Courage.
And courage once
is cowardice another time.
It is only at the moment
that such may be recognized.
The tools and weapons
lie close at hand —
always present, bright and sharpened,
ready for use.
A man outside of men
cultivates each —
stroke for stroke.
Where does one go
without this knowing?
Mischance - mishap —
breathing slight
            or slowly
mention it —
          performance
sleight of hand —
each morning rising
into news of it:

The doom, that sound —
rhythm/ repetitive.
Not the same,
                    the same *at* all.
Always the hammer blow.
Must it be the same hammer?
Blow on the same nail?
Some make it so,
and there is no way back
or out of it.
Do not try it away or outside
of basic illusions.
We are nothing without them.
No one follows easily,
nor leads,
                    lacking belief
which has no actual substance,
but is beyond,
contains all of it.

It was in a dream
-not quite a dream.
I saw them standing
on the earth —
not quite there —
a few men, or were they?
As I came towards them,
a flame leapt out of the grass
and held me for a moment —
frightened me.
Yet I knew I could not live without it.
When it had passed,
the men were gone —
but I kept on climbing
over the parched hillock,
towards the sun,
which hung, at noon,
directly over it.
Shell,
            into and over it.
The dream expands.

The Interlocutor:
That which foretells. That also is the summation.

So, it is rooted here,
cored and centered
in such a way
that nothing may escape it.
Past misgivings —
foregoings, as they may be,
forgiveness before the need.
It is flawed some places,
yet it is solid,
an imperfect shape,
yet one to reckon with.

History, in the telling,
is a blight —
forced across a page —
straitened —
             a wooden thing —
hardly to be thought of
unless in contempt.
His story is something other.
If it has been cultivated,
it loses flavor.
The texture is wild.
It is a freedom,
and it is not thought
                 out.
Taught or fraught,
the rhyming is false
to any ear.
So brings our doom
down to itself.
There is no ease
without its balance
-a noticing
           cursory-
yet decisive.
Make of it the shape.

The Interlocutor:
It is only in old age, or at a time when the spirit is

tempered by what we associate with as the province of
age that a man can understand what clarity and
melody really are. Much that seems meaningless,
disjointed and clouded earlier comes clear at last.

Challenge the sun,
if you will walk there;
it takes that challenge,
and yet a tempered challenge.
No spear thrust
                rends the flames.
The molten tip
                drops,
and becomes one with them,
unsharpened and lost.
(It flows like speech,
in speech — the poem
speaking, into us.
It is not lost
despite its silence.)
Break in the space —
do not defy that other —
challenge in another placing
of the odds.
Step by step
                up
step and
        step
or step - the sound-
judgement, be it challenge,
judgement at the stakes.
Take in an ordering.

The Interlocutor:
It is not good to amass, unless the intention is to use
all that has been saved, and that the using has been
foreseen as a necessity. There is no joy in hoarding.
When the last of what has been assembled is exhausted,
if there is a feeling of joy, then the impulse that
gathered was justified, even though the use leaves a
man in poverty, and apparently without resource. If
this is not the case, then it was an act of selfishness in
no way justified. We 'go empty' at the last of it, naked

and uncomfortable, and if we do not, we are worthless,
and in a state of decay.


The temptation exists,
and it is one to heed.
If the men seen on the road
are not asked,
there will be no answer.
All of this: simplistic,
and yet so difficult.
In the morning,
what was merely shadow
-something seen tentatively-
against a window,
half mirrored,
something further
                    of the light,
and objects beyond
become more solid,
reified.
            I must go there —
and that is beyond an impulse.
It is not a temporary message
given for the moment.
It must be seen as whole,
edged,
            but not a discontinuous edge.

What of the chronicles?
What do they tell me?
that the water in Farmer Giles' pond
will drown me?
That is history.
                    Plunge in.
It is not the teaching
                    this way —
not his/story.

Is it important to establish identity
at the outset?
(The circumstance has
little to do with it.
Call, call to the little stone.)

It is not fixed,
nor is it
        immoveable.
Daylight, daylight,
be not fixed,
            and fixed.
What we have made
-of air and blood —
-fire and salt
and water —
*made —* .
            The silence

drops.

        The Interlocutor:
        Spaces and reiteration. Echo. There is no silence.
        History can be rewritten in any way that you please.
        His/story cannot.


Oiled and precise —
head of the bird —
a stray beside the sea,
returning —
            sense of story —
his - and what he came from.
Air and blood and
fire/salt,
and water - nothing left
to quench it.

        The Interlocutor:
        Despite the claims of many, it is still necessary to set
        up a primal premise in order to move. Let that
        premise be one of love — lived, not preached.


Daily, they reclaim the past —
salvage of detritus —
boards and bottles —
bits thrown out
            (and properly).
Treated with reverence —
nothing but the sense of age —
nothing to be done

but classify.
(Do you see that bird
above us — ?
         Carrion
feeds him —.

Fleshed out —
the motion of a ghost
made palpable —
the tread of bones
propped up.
At night, the sea sounds.
Traffic in memories —
a buoy:
        "Too soon - too late"
The sound of work —
*that* history —
but no one wants the work.
There is no wisdom shared —
as such, it belongs, always,
to the adventurers —
grizzled beards,
thick necks.
A scanning eye —
the men who stand alone,
but not as ads.
There is no Marlboro Country.

We set ourselves,
and leave ourselves.
The world will never be the same again —
but that is instantaneous,
and as it has been,
        always.
The means to make or remake —
make and break.
Foolhardy not to take notice.
Worse, to try to hold it.
The flame is a fish
        in the hand.

Call - call - the set and point —
may as well
        be one word

as another.
Any beginning is the first and
last of it.
Take the start, but do not say
it starts.
(No world we know —
and yet we did.
Whatever we can say
is said within it.
Mix and set are make
and made.
Do not, in such, come fearful.
Whatever we have known,
we have known early.
The latitude is simple —
set by dead reckoning —
all that we deduced
                    we found
fixed.
There is nothing more.
In all
        there cannot be.
It sums, and as the sum
is call.
        (Sea buoy
                offshore.


### 3.


Ama -the mistress of the house —
-soul of the place —
who holds the keys.
Who lives at center,
radiates throughout.
                    Ama.
The truth of the matter.

> The Interlocutor:
> He has said he has been where he has not been —
> partly a lie, and partly arrogant comparison. It is the
> record of many men's lives — yet quality in the telling
> will have made it so or not so.

Figures of men: erotic
or winged —
left running naked on
naked rock.
              "Each winter
the high water and the ice
grind them down a little more.
Well, they'll last as long as I do."
Ama - the soul - the love -
spiritus/inspiritus —
inseparable from what we do.
But, mark it, how always,
the ceremonial marks and magic
are put a little way
from the place of living —
not separate, but a way off.
The lares and penates are gods,
but lesser gods,
              and counted lesser.
Nymphs and dryads
do not live in high temples.
Who says, 'I have been there.'?

    The Interlocutor:
    Voice of the seer is the voice possessed in madness —
    often where the moon travelling between clouds, and
    the sleep of one possessed, places its seal of its color
    on the sleeper's lips. He rises surrounded, not know-
    ing, but his voice outlasts the many phases of a rising,
    dying reflection. He sees in/to.

    Some men, on rising from their dreams, come into a
    life where all impressions are made new — naive —
    fresher and more intense, as if the spirit has regained
    a primal innocence, very briefly. And, indeed, it may
    be true.

Two faces of it:
Travelling,
            the moon has passed
directly between these clouds,
and where I lie —
the madness of the color

on my lips
-a mark- no heat
persistent,
        long beyond that time,
it travels in the grey
of shadows,
        numbed and silent,
to where I burn
from having known it.

Wherever the sun lies,
light is evident.
Where it is dark,
        light was.
The heat of blood
or salt - the burning rocks
of silence.
        Wherever the sun lies
is now - did - is not.

Answer, and flicker of answer,
the echo,
        ripple —
place that was a pressure.
Present? Now?
It must be placed
against the different hours.
At some of them
        we are alive
to what we are not at others.
Bored into,
        sweet and sour
depend upon their own light and dark.
In a fury of talk —
the wisdom lost
-somehow required-
the circuitous route —.

Ah, there is no answer.
Let us go on asking questions.
A sympathy in motion.
Stasis
        also

moves.
Breaking and opening —
the full egg given.
No solution.
Clarity in that.
No, there is no way out.
Fly in the bottle —
wing sound magnified.
I tire of anecdotes,
when there is a story,
often a story in fracture:
high art/high life.
Finally subsumed in fable.
Myth, and of the structure,
myth/ethos.

What was lost in the garden,
becomes the instrument beyond it,
numbed and frozen —
lost — but found once more.
A tool, not an artifact.

**I Ching**

**Missa Solemnis**

The sui —
          following.
Unfolding what is given —
one note to another —
there is nothing to be done
except to follow.
Steer and be steered.
The helmsman follows.
The current prophesies,
and makes good.
Well, in that direction —
It is of the conquered, always,
as he swallows the victor.
The imposed imposes only
what it seeks to destroy.
No change.
The weather clears,
making for another storm.
Who else comes?
What way is opened
that was not open.

The opened vein —
a gout of blood.

    The Interlocutor:
    It is not my business to interpret. It comes only as I
    record, and I record very little. Most of it is repetition.

Then put it on the line.
Nothing but a piece of string.
Few things will stretch,
and nothing stays as straight.
The curve of things is life,
and life begins
            in curve —
circumference of space.
There is no way to avoid it.
Go through.

    The Interlocutor:
    The mark is never what we designate the mark to be.
    The persona is in the river, not the town that bears its
    name as designation.

Oh then, continuance,
as if sound moved itself
around —
         came back
without an echo —
as if a continuity were found,
once more a force
coherent and continuous
with all around it.
Its past no separation
from its place in fact.
This will not do in
by repetition.
Nothing is repeated,
unfolding the long scroll.

    The Interlocutor:
    The heat of what men do is no real heat. — a reflected
    shimmer at the best — arrant bragadoccio at the worst.
    I do not know where one begins, and the other
    ends — beginning being on both sides.

The restless reflection —
these clouds peeled
above us.
A long way —
long and regretful.
Now sees a man,
precisely at the point
of being one,
go in
        deeper?
Reflection and clouds,
a rare morning
when the eyes focus immediately
-do not have to adjust
to the light — by stages.
Making out of it,
a solid comes,
but that is memory —
hardly a thing used —
or known before it has passed.
Some of us try.
Few gain the way.
Mention is made —
but it is mention of facade.
The masonry lies deep,
unseen.

Water-fallen/risen
since we left.
It is not the same
-a single level-
reaches/rises/falls —
is water reaching
where there is no water.
Nothing to receive
if the recognition is not there.

That restlessness
will never allow a place
other than the first place,
from which no one moves
without a place earlier placed.
The victim moves himself,

and finds no movement.
What he thinks he does
receives expression elsewhere.
What is efficient one day
dies the next.
But there is nothing lost —
a norm is reached.
A man stays on
in surprising context —
from nurture to what he is.

The Interlocutor:
There comes a time when a man is in a position to
have all that he has wanted, but of course, he no
longer wants anything by the time he has reached that
place. It is almost axiomatic that at the moment he is
granted his wish, he has gone away on a fishing trip,
and can't be reached.

As at the turn of a great number,
we might stay there:
Centuries/millennia.
All of it will be done
without a sense of us,
our sense coming only
as we arise.
Not to be niggardly, but
the number kept and realized,
puts a man on his way,
and his is the only one.
No other path, trail, or road.
Hateful terms!
We want more than we can have.
The body settles in
at a point —
that point goes on.
It is not a quest —
it is only the way for one body —
corporation.
How much can be held there.
Counting all the losses,
nothing is heaven.
It might as well be the gain.

A soundless, wet morning —
late in the year,
and the books are open
to wet pages.
Nothing that was written there,
looks well, though it is the same
I saw there in sunlight.
It is not duty,
nor self-congratulation.
Pity's the same.
It is no way out —

**Abnaki directions for the** yet it pulled us in
**balance of a birch bark** -the weight-
**canoe** 'as a leaf on water.'

The Interlocutor:
To circumscibe the limits is not necessarily parochial,
nor is it to forget other, but distant, antecedence. It is
merely an allowance: that specific land may support
its own without adulteration, and with the fullest use
of what that land can supply. There are few places
where the problem is not relevant, and must be faced
eventually. What is there, appaently passive, conquers
the most absolute of conquerors.

The arrogance which set sail
was of, and with, the man.
He could not be other
than he was,
but set a reaction
we live with, still.
A malign breath across these waters —
not the waters' will.
A veer in willing —
always a belief that what is to be found
is further off-
— a little.
*One* stands and says,
'Pick it up.'
No one listens.
(A few, in a hard time —
the pinch.)
Hardly worth the time.

The cry comes,
            surely,
nailed secure, into the skull,
tried most against the young:
Indoctrination.
'Falsify! Falsify!'
They must not know.
It is for the common good."
a common
            weal
(as weal is wound)
and another:
            "Debunk it."
Neither bears on *his* story.
Sometimes the fresh naivete
whips mastery
into the ground.
Not always,
            there stands a chance
Whatever do I
            -have-
moved against.
No longer caring for the face —
pressed —
against the glass.
We know some words for that —
pariah, only one.
Is it one I do not care about?
or is it self?
contained in self?
A richness asks.
It is no asking for the riches.
Further inland,
across this isthmus.
'a ways from here.'
far piece.
An echolalia.

And sea —
            the restlessness —
the track ploughed in.
Take portion
            -what is carried-

always as the burden.
Let it go —
scanting the tips of fingers —
as the wave
         edge on.

    The Interlocutor:
    And I have heard through other sources what is harsh:
    A word that no man wishes.


The land will no longer
support your houses.
They will collapse
into their cellar holes
              unused
and stillborn —
          pockmarks
upon the older ground,
to fill with water.
Seep and erode untried,
into the contours and bones
of the earth.
So much untried
that does not destroy itself.

    The Interlocutor:
    And what I have heard comes muffled on a wet
    morning. It is so wet that clothes and papers stick — the
    fronds and leaves of the plants each hold a bead of
    water — still there is no rain to assuage the thirst.


The sea, always the sea,
restless in
put
    out
tress kelp combed
back again
           mark
on rock
        indented
shores
     a
float.

The Interlocutor:
Hear that voice! Believe!

Heaved off the flood
(why *that* verbiage to mind —
no matter)
                    is, and rests
as it is,
            may never
move in other circles
than the wake —
or some small piece of flotsam
caught in tow, and now
left far behind.
They have smelled the blood
of living,
                    indistinguishable
from salt of spray,
dark night at sea,
when wind is all about —
abroad the deep.

We often hear those voices,
and then must leave them
far ashore —
                    athwart —
lost in the shouts of the drowned,
or rocks that drag their moorings
on a shingle ledge,
drawn out in each successive swell.
Clamor arises:
the inner, romantic,
against the outer
cut edges of cold light —
above —
                    and seeming —
constant.
No wonder in it,
more than ranging —
heaves the sea —
and thirst for savor of it.
They come to this advantage,
then have left us

to our own deserts.
Bend sail and search.

> The Interlocutor:
> It is a bright day when some small and perfect object
> is discovered, or rediscovered. There is no difference.
> Often these things which we reject, or tolerate, merely
> because of what we feel is their commonness — that
> they are heard or seen too often — achieve their
> greatest importance through that commonness. Exact-
> ly that, no more nor less. It is their totality.

And from the mistakes —
tragedy or glory.
Praise or blame rests aside.
What one does with it
becomes another affair.
Much to be undone,
and nothing assuages —
wound and fire.
Such wounds and scars
go otherwise,
subsumed in an alembic
strange to us —
often missed.
They mutate.
Return to us:
Ama — mistress of the house —
soul of the place.
And hold the key,
even to the heading
in what is season.

And in those islands
there was little want.
A large population
lived in peace and friendship.
"Twenty persons working
but six hours a day
for one month
will make a planting
of such conuces
that will provide bread

**Bartoleme de Las Casas
in the *Apologetica***

of three hundred persons
upwards of two years."
"The plants grown
were neither demanding
Nor exhausting of soil fertility."
(Laid waste by arrogance
and stupidity
in less than twenty years
by the freebooters at Espanola.
Where is Ama?
Their word?

'Sail on!', indeed.)
A travesty of sea and land
by those incompetent
on one as in the other.
Discovery equals destroy.
Slave and penal colonies.
Trip on the earth again.
Kiss, with a broken mouth
Kiss, with a broken mouth.
What does ill at home
rarely prospers elsewhere.
Avarice, grandmother of usury,
set fires that still burn.
Little cools in those middens —
the split skulls
beside broken dreams,
and shattered men.
Leave them to sleep.
Potsherds lie sharp
in unequal grounds.
Set aside no days
for celebration —
none for weeping.
Walk alone, and cursed
across the deserts.
There is something other —
how
        to
express - it
comes in short spurts —
a pressure clogged

and waiting.
There is no season
further than this one.
They are all-
        -one.

    The Interlocutor:
    It does no good to talk of those things which cannot be
    helped — if they are evil or benign — a man walks
    slowly according to the light/reflection of just those
    stones lying at his feet. It is a fate. The only one.


As he made the ascent
over the little hill
-swelling of the upland fields-
there was something caught.
He felt a constriction,
                first,
and then it happened:
as if the heat had crushed
together —
          a ball of fire
exploding in a wind of molten violence
next his ear.
He heard it,
yet did not hear.
Felt what he could not feel.
It was the presence of spirit,
and he was sure that he would die.
Yet he did not die.
He stood there on the slope,
swaying perilously
for only a moment.
It was finished —
and he went on
          outwardly
as if nothing had happened.
Yet he had lived
all ages at once,
and he could not come down —
ever - or again.
This was the mark —
the seal of the only doom.

The Interlocutor:
When a man speaks most fully, he speaks in blood.
There is no heard voice in it.

Next to the skin, a talisman,
a shard of the earth —
nothing made by others.
It is a beginning —
where they found the means.
The incitement:
the tools, later,
                    crafted.

**Eagle Island**  On some island beach,
   **8/19/77**  a splintered rock
later washed into form.
From that, the awl.
Or something flat for planes.
Things of beauty —
jewel and ornament
in the taking —
                    always the use.
Blood ritual.
                    Return.
Placed in the midst
of such as this must be,
there is no choice left.
His story falsified,
we are given history.
The fruitfullness of earth
leaches out.
More is taken,
                    none returned.
Many are called —.
In the torn wrecks,
something of the spirit.
Magnificence haunts,
but is shy to appear.
What was once,
cannot be.
Thinking takes the place
-apology-

few care to flaunt
against it.

> The Interlocutor:
> Nothing has come into this world — bitter or sweet. It
> is a process of ripening. Only, after many days, and
> suns, can it be known as outcome — whether it is to be
> prized or shunned.

Easily reached, that day,
yet, from it, harder to break loose.
As the descent of the mountain
is always more perilous
than climbing up.
Few mention this.
Perhaps they feel no sense
of accomplishment.
It is so,
        cleaning up
after the holocaust.
It is not exciting —
yet far more noble.

> The Interlocutor:
> If a man loses his shadow, the sunlight is useless to
> him. He will weaken and die — and if not sooner,
> then, later. In the clearest pool of water, he sees no
> reflection. It is high time he flees from himself.

And this is the founding of the maelstrom:
for all of the motion and violence
outside,
        there is none in.
It is so with cyclone —
from the center,
                flies apart,
leaves only
        -generative-
a book in sand.
Laid waste,
or how the waste might come.
Their children grow in ashes.
Gently,
        decay might bring a strength,

but this is bitter —
acrid to all senses.
Sense of being —
count it out.

The taint stays in the blood,
and spreads.
It is not only those of us
descended from the responsibility.
Everywhere,
                      and in that
which we tyrannize.
A cut in the arm
                              tasted:
blood is bitter.
Daylight transcends it,
but only for a moment.
We are darkened.
Yet a certain defiance
mitigates the darkness.
To look it squarely in the teeth:
That will do it,
and that is his story.

    The Interlocutor:
    It must come as caution. nothing 'pays.' There is no
    redemption. Rectitude posited above deceit is still a
    falsehood.

Too much realized,
and never enough.
The men at Espanola
are at work among my apples.
Whatever I pick up,
the sadness,
                      gnarled and bitter —
The Asian malus.
Where a footprint,
the foot has been.
Spoor is hot.
The pursuing armies follow,
and there will be retribution,
senseless as what began it.

Then, to compromise
makes it all plain.
We have no home here,
and never had.
Why should we pretend to it?

And when the spring begins to fail
in a wet season —
winds and rain
following the coast
as usual — the time of year —
there is wonderment.
Few go deep enough
to find the roots buried
in the earth —
cut and bruised, and poisoned.

    The Interlocutor:

    Time passes from the fourth to the fifth world. There
    is no altering the shape of it.

Next to whatever I can pick up,
what is left behind me —
that nothing is lost.
A hindsight on the place
which has lost so much —
one is tempted to say,
                    everything,
though there is much
yet to be accounted —
but —
where the grapes no longer
trail in the tide.
Not the numbers of men
— there were men there,
long prior —
the kinds of men.
These who strive and wrestle,
fail —
        pull down in their thunder,
much that does not live by stress.

**Pascal**    Quiet men, in quiet rooms.

The Interlocutor:

But I would be more than a cautionary figure. I am
not father to this world. I take it, rather, that as Rabbi
Tarphon said, "It is not given me to finish the work,
but neither may I desist from it." And that my function
is that of a Pimen in his monastery cell, attempting to
record his story — a stream of coherent events out of
conflicting accounts.

Now and then the restlessness of wind —
the ends striking and stirring
far from the sources —
a fresh gale
somewhere off to sea.
It can be quiet
for all of the sounds
locked somewhere in space —
as nothing is lost, wholly,
not clamor, or joy.
Still, the angle of hearing
deflects to source,
and will not be chained
to usury and spoils.

Then,
          something does give benison,
though few care to hear
that far,

          or see —
or partake of ritual.
men?
          Not always men.
Life in other things.
Forms not dreamed of,
voices not pitched or placed
for us.
We contemplate —
think too much.
Out from Espanola,
the sun does shine —
and plenteous.

## 4.

Whoever has pursued his death,
has been pursued
-pursuit as process-
has become the ideal
-stifled at times-
and bare of thought.
it is the shadow
seen at night
beyond the circle of a campfire
-if a fire is safe.
He is, for *he* is spirit,
telling and urging,
a supremacy —
weightless,

        on march,
in saddle,
a sailor with the others,
or sitting across a table
where his company
has worked

        and eaten.
We are various,
but we are in agreement
-not our own-
another's.

        But is is not
a haunt —

        and knowing
may not deter a victim.
Degrees of strength,
arbiter and no arbiter.

As if a screen of vision
were channelled —
divided by a mountain.
Blurred or distorted,
it may or may not return.
It is not a trick
-no optics-
It must, and will, lead
to decisive cleavage.

A cataclysm,
in which everything
-the unseen as well-
is reformed
upon that dark and bloody ground
of birth and death.
A solid floor to bear them —
these who follow.

At whatever point
the watch stops,
there is a time.
The flow leaks in —
and around it.

Whatever there is
can be picked up
anywhere.
To disprove it,
disproves nothing.
nor in the visible flow —
a sweep in circling
at a measure —
is there any part of time.

      The Interlocutor:
      Whoever I am, I do not feel that I am called upon by
      usual means. it is not a prophecy, but a means to live.

A tragedy of age:
that in its wisdom
-for want of it-
it will no longer sieze on
anything but what remains
a familiar.
Knowing the falsehood
-interpretation-
it goes back, nevertheless,
in nostalgia, and sticks,
confuses a put down
with the stream.
It can't be helped —
merely a sadness.

Putting together such things,
a face begins to show itself
out of broken glass —
and it is not one face
so much as type —
                    at first,
then clears and cools,
sharp and distinct.
It is the type,
and it is also one
-unique-

A man outside himself,
yet collected.
it is of this
            the metal refines,
drops away from slag,
                    molten,
cools into resolve —
noble or base by weight,
often some of each.
To be put behind/ahead
in any season
                    may force the bloom,
and that bloom will lose
in scent and color,
except it come by itself.
This is the secret
nothing is a 'right'
by rights.
What is taken, comes to be
in right taking.
The virtues reaffirm,
only from themselves —
they are not property.
Our thought will not stay them.
Figures of such men,
artless and timeless,
they are not in charge.
A wordless voice
-their prompting-
urges them, and
at the highest moments

they despair,
                    each time
they glimpse the power
in their helplessness.
Something is wrenched out —
perhaps the soul itself,
staked in a dying wind,
unable and inept,
pursued in all pursuit.
Admitted or not,
becomes the death.

    The Interlocutor:
    But there is singleness, and purpose out of singleness.
    It is/is not. Illusion becomes palpable — is not illusory.

A keepsake in the desert —
meeting — plan of strategy.
The fate converges
on its subject.
Whispering, that most defiant act,
take up the bulk of the journey,
onto a shoulder,
heaved there —
another bag of ration.

There is talk of cruelty —
little that serves it
other than self-service.

There is no retribution
other than the hand
against itself.
Of all things made,
there is endurance
only in the search.
Belief is in it —
is a part of it —
in the end may be the whole,
the rest having fallen away,
detritus of the long journey.
In solitary measure,
each man must find
the journey — endurance for it —

how to compose the hands
that they do not strike each other.
Balance and revise —
how we mean to live,
and do not live,
                    save in the moments
closest to the bone.
Nothing is put upon us
outside ourselves,
that we do not put there first.
We mark ourselves —
ashes and chalk —
the battle paints.

Out of ignorance,
a knowledge,
                    supple,
tough as withe —
fibre that will hold.
Knowledge?
                    Easy to acquire,
if allowed to come
in its own season.
The severity of teaching is
much overrated.
The season brings ripeness,
and it is not by rote.

    The Interlocutor:
    I have looked in, and seen nothing. That is the final
    clarity. By that, I have made myself open.

Prompted by something outside.
Animus?
            No,
animus is not beyond a place.
Recognition:
Eat what the land affords.
This is what the land affords.
This is the opening
and the spirit.
Not in depair —
                    one cannot.

'Senor General, there is no more money.'
'So?'
            'Then we will print some.'
If one uses false specie,
any falsehood will do
to cover it.
Place belief in it —
so much complains within complaint.
To the letter of what one finds,
if it cannot be explained
to be another thing.
This is the only wisdom
at the beginning,
and with that pry
to turn it over,
and make it for something else.
They reasoned within
and for themselves —
made nothing other.
Perhaps it is only one year
-a poor season-.
                    Nothing yields
beyond its own seed.
But there are other years —
and we must live
into them.
One way is one way,
and there are various.


        The Interlocutor:
        How many regrets are stifled in loneliness. How much
        of it breaks out in the cold sweat of old age? It is
        useless to pursue this. Too many regrets. Instinctual
        as birds — the home harbinger.


Any man might say
that he would be doing
things other than he does,
if he had a choice (chance)
                        just one.
But if had done anything
other than what he did do,

he'd be doing other
than he is. Right now.
Chain of events,
and as simple as a simple chain.
That quick — and the sum total
would be the same.
Always is.
So few — so few of us —
the inane excuse,
and yet another few
take to the background,
and make it, quietly,
what it is.
There is nothing blurs there
save in the eye unfocused.
Pursued,
              that last ambition
is the first one.
It is named for death.
It is an equal.
No matter, then.
Tipped into the doing —
do it all.

Treadmills and threshings —
these for the winnowings.
grain succumbs but conquers.

The journals of working and sleeping.
Shouldn't a man
pay as much attention
to one as the other?
It is the bravery of our time
that any will attempt it.
Many laugh.
It is a portion of the time
stays this.
And from that portion, ours,
not a spin off —
reified —
              a gaining.
Well then,
              if a man

dies in the process,
he does not die —
knowing the levels of himself —
always dead,
and always living —
there is not the cleavage —
passage from one to the other.
It is once or twice
that a man
                rises,
or that he falls.
Too much made
of what is little.
Defend or depart
from where or what
he is/is not.

> The Interlocutor:
> It was a close beginning. It will be a close end. No one
> can reach beyond that — yet all men attempt it, and in
> a partial assay, they talk of miracles.

From this into anger —
ramified — a personal zeal —
the rationale
from which act begins.
The beginning is a compromise —
no beginning
and little ending.
(Bent into the wind,
where is he going?
What is the errand?
Implacable as revenge
-but not that-
something other —
ravening the gut,
lean from little sustenance,
a hunger which leads away
beyond horizons —
looking back to this one.
Now there is little left
for argument.

It is a secret way —
and the journals kept
more private than the dust
hidden in old corners.

That which is addressed to emptiness,
will not reach it.
If there is an empty place,
it is denied a man,
and when he goes there
it will no longer be empty,
or open to his singleness.
He has brought his armies
with him.
       The solitude is broken
-and never was-
         An idea.
Only that much.
We spend our time
thinking chimaera.
Each pinch of dust
has made us,
and will go from us.
The spring freshet comes unbidden,
dies, and cracks the mud
with no more added to it.
Broken open,
       this loneliness —
a fact of disease —
nothing more.
Address that emptiness, and
be damned.

    The Interlocutor:
    I must suffer all of this, and break my own silence —
    only enough to hear the sound of my own voice.
    Sounds, sounds, preface more sounds. They do not
    dissipate.

Carry across to the new page.
The mark is already on it.
We trace what we do not know —
thinking that we create

what we cannot find.
Breaking loose,
the solemn mark
another form of dancing,
light and inconsistent.
The measure tips and spills
at the moment it is full.
We know it all
before we learn it,
and in learning, lose
the best of it.
Broken loose again,
the sound scuds —
a free sail
in the wind —
clocked to the blood —
as the blood pressures from it.
Take hold.
Do not presume.

As of a voice,
singing in its clarity:
"The arrow on the path
is a semblance —
a cleavage
between directions.
It is purpose —
not substance,
and there is no other
reasoning.
        No wall
between right and left."

Whatever chance there might be,
stays in the earth.
The man shows only
as a part of it.
It is the actual portion,
chained and bound
to darkness —
        clangor
of the gate closed behind him.
It is no more than for the others

walking a little way in sunlight.
Prime mover never was.

A fan of light
under the door
to let in something —
let something out.
It is particular,
and hard and dangerous.
It raises the mask
of the disguise
                    (not the disguise
itself)
and allows the entrance
of danger —
a simple exit of the light.
Who is the man
we talk of?
What did he do?
His story?
We come to all of that —
but later on.
It is a mistake
to propose more than this,
or even tell his story,
unless we are a part of it.
But we are that part
which carries
in ceremony and ritual
the story,
                    and the future
of the story.
Upwards from the years,
we have made time in it,
and it is the only making —
the discovery.

> The Interlocutor:
> It is not hard to place all of this, despite its meander-
> ings. But it is folly to attempt to step across the
> bayous — to go from here to there, unless we follow
> the current. It is more than a different journey, and
> in places it is no journey at all.

Half of the part
of the past
may be over.
In its precision,
it is an obdurate
opening into and beyond
its pressure.
We have talked enough,
and yet we never talk enough.
There is a weight
that must be lifted,
and can only lift
in being.
Words must carry over —
stand as bridge
between the parts of living.

**Pancho Villa**
**c. 1894**

"Still a boy,
he preferred being
a successful bandit
to seeing his family dishonored."
What were the means
to honor or dishonor?
Could he know
that one stolen horse
would change his life?
had through dishonor
translated him
                    to
something far greater,
though many still deny it?
Fixing his purpose,
he set out.

"It is my fate to suffer.
Give me your blessing,
commend me to God, and
He will know what to do."
(But not to escape a burden
of one's own.
                    It is a way,
to ask for one companion
on a perilous journey.

641

Perhaps an idea:
                    God
(or God's)
a talisman.

A mastery from sources
-disparate-
It is hard for those concerned
with what is contextual
in usual terms
to fit the pieces.
All right, let it be.
The life is not lived
to make a pattern for
critics.
We take what we can use
from any source —
to hell with consequence.

It is not fashionable
except when fashion coincides,
and that is in snatches —
no pattern at all,
and nothing to make one.
(Grace to remember that.
There are times when fashion removes.
Others, when a man
must stand and bear ridicule.
If we live at all,
we live alone.)
What a man says in his sleep,
may not prove,
                    often,
the man,
            but there are times
when it does.
"If I do not understand
the terms in which you ask,
how can I do what you ask,
even if it is a thing I could do?"
I heard that,
            and the man
-in revolt-

                    fleeing first,
then,
                    the sweat of what he felt.
Fighting more and more alone,
the lordly and the isolate.
a tablature given over
to many meanings —
as simple as one stone —
one leaf —
or a thread on water —
as complex.
Straighten the line.
The way is open to you.
Opens.
a sense of logic,
balance and gravity,
which is personal.
Will, for a season,
carry the man on —
iron rations in the desert,
but there is nothing personal
to save beyond himself,
unless a conviction,
twisted at root,
that he serves the others.
Those who have no voices.
On that bias,
anything becomes a possible.
It is the vein and marrow
of a heritage.
Kings who were kingly
lived in bondage.
"I went with him
into his own country,
and was amazed."
There is no time
that does not need this,
sense of a calling —
that it be for all of them,
more than whim —
a calling.
let them call, and be called.

The Interlocutor:
So we step one side — away from morality. It is clear
that no true thing is in societal vengeance. Break
open all the prisons. We have no right to hold
hostages, or to detain one man inside.

The properties of light
are as the vision:
each man seeing it —
not light, but what it lightens.
It is a slow passage
for each of us,
to realize this,
and in the realization,
to talk of mirrors,
not of the light itself,
which no man sees,
or only in that short day
when power has left him,
and the final journey has begun.
Any, and into the source.
To dissolve into the parts once more.
It is in these parts,
                              no will,
and none to be.
The sun and moon will
generate another combination.
"My indignation was brief.

**Pancho Villa, confronted**
**by Huerta's firing squad**

It changed to sorrow.
The men for whom I have been fighting,
wish to kill me."
It is easy to bend one's fears
into righteousness.
To sweat of work
-its own contempt upon it-
dismisses all except those
who stand shoulder to its own.
"chocolate drinkers."
"Sweet-scented friends."
Dismisses and goes on.
So it comes to cases:
Integrity is that

which stems from one man —
what he believes.
From any of us as men
conviction carries into right.
Equal/opposed
                    is stalemate.

"The honor of marriage is there,
and that of love is here."
This is the rationale —
what keeps the animus,
allows the man to walk
scot free.
                    (Is *root* free.)
through perilous association.
There can be no final judgement,
but I will stay with each man,
holding to what he knows
as true to what he is.

It is a distance,
                    middle or far,
the power of forms
is a single one.
In that place
                    (as case)
looking from a distance,
such a circle
makes the straight
a curve beside it.
It is a fiction,
and not
            a fiction.
The least of it
breaks the wall
between all shapes.
We die on difference —
the smug indifferences —
no matter what the focus
may have said.
It is the pressure
of a theory.
Impressed,

                bound to the ear —
such galleys on the sea.

The roughest stone,
covered in ivy,
softens —
marked in its duty
to enclose.
Those within, stare out
framed in a gardening
not their own.
The inner flame burns on.
Basic contentions
when there is no basis.
All of it shifts on whim.
A permafrost until the thaw.
It is another meaning —
one more aspect of his story.
The faces of these men
tell little.
We trust in shadows
and chimaera.
None of them were movers
more than moved.
It delays its action,
until the act,
                long past,
is equally forgotten.
The events are not results of plan.
A poor night's sleep
-one man's-
persists through generations.

        The Interlocutor:
        After periods of waiting which seem no more than
        spaces filled with argument, there is an action — not
        covert — but violent in its evidence. It *seems* that
        everyone died last week, and there is no one left. Still,
        we go on. Next week there will be others — and other
        deaths.

"And when I look
at another man's work —

646

work which pleases me —
wondering why I cannot do
as he has done —
I am answered
                easily
by myself:
                that I am not that man,
and what I do is mine,
in the same measure.
But it echoes in my head
-a sound-
             sticking —
something I have heard before,
Perhaps have spoken aloud
to others.
I do not mind the redundancy
as that much.
I pick up my will,
and go on with it."

It drips outside —
hardly call that rain,
though it is relative,
and in time
                may come to it.
*I* can sit here,
             and think
through smoke of others.
What is the bone of it?
Where is contention
more than contending?
All I have to make it from
is haze and drizzle —
the smoke from an autumn fire.
(Behind the stove,
a wet cloth yellows,
but does not dry —
wick to the roots below it.)
And as it drips,
I turn to other things —
nervous not to be abroad.
Others are,
             have been.

The gist of it:
that some men deny
their tenets to reach
the principle.
I cannot deny them the right.
As one goes deeper
                    into one's self
the cause for outside suspicion
grows.
        Comrades are no longer
comrades.
In the end, we fight alone.
The tempers of the swords differ,
but we are left
                alone,
to deal with that.
No group and no cause
can stand against
one man convinced.

(As ever, with the singe of winter,
light frost in early morning.
It strengthens,
                and the sun
lies heavy on the fruit.
Bone to stick the teeth.

The rationale again:
"How sweet the sound of cannonade,
particularly
              when it is directed
against one's enemies."
And after the executions,
a hearty chicken dinner
under the mesquite.
No conscience, or one in abeyance
for the issue —
only a sense of duty —
one taken higher up.
How high?
The cruelties, and tenderness,
flesh on ligature —
the bone and gristle.

A man is worth the manhood,
judged solely for himself.
Do not prove hasty
in dismissal.
It will ripen in regret.

From Juarez to Zacatecas —
San Luis Potosi.
He ranged far
across the mountains,
in the cities,
pelted and smothered
in flowers of welcome.
Tears of the people.
"Send that boy to college,
or I will have you executed.
I say this, senor,
who cannot read or write,
and daily know the cost."
(Nor should *he* judge,
beyond his single case.

    The Interlocutor:
    You may take it either way, and both are faulty: In
    creating, you make up a possiblity, or use up a resource.

A sadness-
that the young
are the only ones
who are fired by greatness,
and soon learn 'better.'
The true man is a lone one.
Only a few keep to it,
raging in old age.
The fishermen dread east wind
after a few trips —
                lose nerve.
Once in a century,
an old man who sets out
from his household —
like as not to die
in a way station.
But he *does* set out.

Righteousness is no cause,
it is the strength of one
away and against many.
I do not wish to know
the reasons.
Whatever reasons are,
they are not *the* reasons.

A swoon of sleep,
and in that place
the desert winds
blow fitfully:
The final ambush,
and an unsolved death.


5


Clamor of the sea
to be heard again,
over the affairs of those
far inland.
Clamor that raises —
foreshortens and falls.
In the ear,
                    the roar of blood
is sound of wave —
pulse and length —
turning and returning
to origins.
The antecedents lie here.
Roses a mile inland
bloom fainter than those
which catch the spume.
Birds in their hearing,
chart course by surfsound —
a low frequencey
pulsing hundreds of leagues
inland.
            As men, we wither
in the extremities,
away from the sea,
and the littoral margins.

Our riparian rights stripped from us,
diminish,
though many who have had
no experience of water
in themselves,
              do not recognize
the signs of their pining.
The sea,
          as the flood and the neap
of the sea —
          in season-
the sea/ sons.

What traffic there is,
and what commerce —
come in the ships
that are set on the tides —
and move out on the waters,
a way from the land,
yet not away —
              running
towards other land —
the shores continually
rising and falling
out of the water.
It is relative
-not a long way —
if the bend of the life
holds on and into
the salt and the moving
of swell and of wave.
Clamor against it
is small business,
lost in the pulse of it,
closed over and raised again,
marking the shoals and the reefs —
shipwreck and grave.
It was a long time, also,
before the first of us
crawled up on the shores,
and dried off in the sun.
We are sprung loose now.
We think we are loose,

and yet we are bound.
Our very blood is,
in its balance,
little but sea water.
Whatever freedom we have
is as limited a space
as the hours of movement —
one tide
        in/to
another
        tide.
catching and falling —
the stains on the cliffs
and the sand.
To/wards and fro/wards,
flotsam,
        bobbing at temporary anchor
in tide pools,
flushed out in the rise
of the cycle,
next time around.
If we would think of it,
thought of the kind
would cut through
the sense of our 'business',
to take it away,
as if it were nothing —
a contemptible Gordian Knot.
There are few
who will turn this direction —
even the sailors
sail *on* to the sea,
and not in it:
The swim,
        where they do not
attempt a swimming.
It is not enough to live
on the shore,
        or on vacation
to open a picture window
          to it.
It is the force of all living,

and the shell of the past
put to the ear,
                    and the lips.

    The Interlocutor:
    I have built boats of chips and cork, and I have freed
    them, along with ripe leaves, in the channel of our
    river — that eventually they may reach the tide in
    their outward journey. Greater: Other men may pick
    them up, and find use for them, or a simple pleasure.

So it was set
in the uncertainty
of structure —
a figure of fire
that keeps turning
-a part to the part —
and ever itself —
the flow of all water,
failing and falling,
drop by drop —
returned to the sea
from its loan.

A far distance
                    (we made it)
but only our own.
Put off from one shore,
to find another.
We think it a difference,
but that is only in ourselves,
and we are not different
except in category
which we raise
to recognize a shape
-any shape-
as if it mattered.
So much for it then.
One day's work is another's.

Looking for it,
I lose it,
come up with a small answer
which is true paradox:

That things are
exactly what they seem to be —
and that splits reality,
leaving the blade
between its parts —
stuck there to rust —
perhaps to absorb its salts
into both halves,
as there are flowers
which take on color
from metals at the root:
Red for iron —
Blue for copper.
Suspension and reflection —
that it all holds as
the savor of a mothering —
of the amniotic waters.
Storm across these seas:
A *high* suspension.
Preferred in its own wake.

Stride of those men —
broken —
         not the lock step
they imagined it to be.
Set of the camp on an island
contiguous to the shores
they intended to plunder.
**Sir Ferdinando Gorges**    "In Casco Bay —
an island called Damariscove."
(An ordinary gripe
in the bowels
will lead to an assessment:
'Finished in pain.'
But the pain does not fit —
a rumbling somewhere else.)
Intrigue earlier,
turned state's evidence,
the seed of a forty years' attempt
to recoup.
Henchman of the 'Lord's Brethren,'
to furnish:
         "Fish, furs, and timber."

The method left to the proprietor.
Failure, and a final monarchy —
his sign of success.
Ten years on that coast
as a king —
oppressor in extreme.
The vanity of his age.
A shadow story
built on hearsay,
and the final word
from Boston —
that in government,
as in religion,
he was not one of them.
(Little choice in method,
for the assumed difference.)
The monarchy was dissolved,
attached to the Bay Colony,
as 'the maine',
and the wars began —
fought here in fierceness
beyond other places,
and for a longer time.
Time against those shores.
A few old forts,
paving stones worn smooth
in three hundred years of tide,
storm waves to uncover them.
Little left us.
The foundations of settlements
spread along the coast,
pre-empted from those prior.
Death of the forests,
and those who lived there.
For this a man may be accounted
worthy (!)
There is nothing more to say —
no place to stay.
The sea rises
                in a storm
into the trees.

The Interlocutor:
Difficult to find a lead-in here. It is a tantalizing
story — the bones of it — but little to flesh it out except
for the same injustice that ran uniform through the
original conquest and settlement. We have always
wanted to make this stolen land 'safe' for something,
and with signal and uniform failure.

No one around.
The sigh of the wind
in cold sharp enough
to bring blood from the air
itself —
tears from the water.
No place for that
in the planning.
Contempt for what is there.
Bring up a way,
and there will be none.
Stood over and left
to its own device.

Groundwork and openings —
a form of speech
-the implement-
enough for tool to let it be.
The cases opened
-speech for them-
an utterance of
our indictment.
That purity-a sound
which does not cover
wrongs,
            nor rationalize
impression
            of a land
no longer virgin.
"Plenty more where that came from."
And burn the heartwood
with the slash.
The sea reverses
in its wanderings —
slap at the edge of the foam.

And I remember a time
-in swimming-
        when a fish
rose on a wave;
and as the water broke
I called to her:
        'Quickly, catch it.'
And she did.)

Too far, we've come
too far to know
much of what that land was like.
It was not simple then,
but it was not as it is now.
A complexity is not
        always
confused.
And we sit here confused
by what we have confused.
(Quickly,
        catch it,
if there is to be
a thing
        caught.
Out of this - little -
the confusion rises:
Clouds of midges in the spring —
the haze, late summer.
Buried in winter —
the burden of our snows.
A far season for any of us.
We do not know the land,
and parcel it
        for spite.
A fury at ourselves
returns in desperation.
In fair mind
        we destroy
what we have loved.
If it is nothing we can hold,
then, search it
that no one else may have it.
Always the thinking in terms

of our own kind.
Others would like it,
                        too.
It cannot be built on argument,
nor on one species
-true specious argument —
but the words take it
for themselves —
                        and for those.
Our sense of it —
-sense of words —
is faulty, as our sense
of sea and land.
Always with the will
to business.
            It is lost to us
which would be given
                        gladly
with another direction
from us.

     The Interlocutor:
     There was a man who gave up 'gainful' employment
     in mid-winter. he said he would shellfish along the
     tide, and cut firewood — both for his own use — and
     that his earnings would be superior to those he would
     have had from the job. He was accused of 'low aim.'

The installations at York and Popham
were of stone.
The Indians had seen nothing
like them.
The Sunday meetings
were dreary,
but they came
out of fear and curiosity.
(They built of stone —
                        homes
and fortifications,
and the roads between them,
left to wash
in the higher tides.
The sea casts up its fish

to gasp and die
beyond its reach —
one man and many marks
incised on rocks
worn down to sand
-an increment-
the sedimentary culch and fossil
bedded in the clay.

This hard and dreaming shore —
its blend of goodness
                          with its usury
and curse —
                patina on the old
amoral rock which does no more
than front the elements
as it did —
                beneath a dressing.
Flesh has been mistaken for it.
It is not the flesh.
Nor can we bring it life —
no breathing in —
inspirit.
Arrogance may seem by force
to do what is no force.
No living thing.

(I thought, this day,
to come there earlier
than I did —
but not along the rivers
-east-
            to catch that sun
-a gilding —
and forget the men I knew:
hewers of wood,
                   cutters of stone,
who fouled the courses and the tides
on every reach
                around me.
The high seas had their say.
And the men left shards enough,
but sunk in backwash and spindrift.

Hard to find,
                    without the eye for it.
Perhaps perverse —
                    the elation
in a stone chip
exhumed from proper burial.

The resources
Fur, fish and timber —
exported to the Old World,
where the like had not been seen
in many centuries —
a burned out land
attempting life
grafted on new vigor.
Renewable resource,
had it been understood —
destroyed and lost
in those first years —
the sources rooted out.
Gorges and his boon companions
carousing in a keep —
their wealth in specie —
coin they could not spend,
nor well refuse,
once entered on the track.

Sea birds, as on the land,
proclaim themselves
bright autumn days.
We do survive them
in their salt —
                    remove
again,
        or lighten,
feel them,
                    touching —
benison of seasons —
place to close the year.
And yet we did no good thing
surmounting —
a besting —
we have known

no creature comfort
                         other.
What we have made ourselves
in specious case,
and earned in usury.
All through that history,
the settling,
                         mud and silt.
There is no capstone.
The story continues
wavering,
                         and an attempt
at repetition.
Thence!

The speech is mixed,
and there is no purity
from it, back to other uses.
It is no place for a man,
and yet the man lives there
surrounded by its clutter.
The compass in that mist,
hung with skulls,
pierced by thorns.
A winding horn
to cut it.
The cry of the heroes
is always a similar,
but the clearing comes
only in old tales.
(Next to the tale
its revival —
the uses updated.
The despair turns in on itself,
and faith, abused,
the only clearing.
A slow ascent,
only to find that the way
is other:
In/out/around.

Looking up quickly,
I mistake his flag

Gereint, Son of Erbin
(Mabinogion)

661

for the man.
A strange mistake,
and yet the most common.
We live in these worlds
of association —
most of them false,
and yet coherent,
to the place they solidify
in conceit and tradition.
How often do we see the man?
It is not merely a passing glance
out to a child's fort
in late October.
Off, in a portion of dream,
where no one thing
supports another.
Not to *go* on,
yet we go.
A tension, as equinox —
particular
        in the places
to sense what is,
and what is not —
that what we come away with
is the space.
The men of history
are surrounded by that space,
and it is more than they are.
Freighted with his story,
it holds up —
both itself, and whatever else
may be emptied into it.
It is the far cry,
and it is the near echo —
buzzing of the breath
        and pulse.

    The Interlocutor:
    It is in giving up, not giving up at the same time, that
    one reaches an 'end.' There is no victory either side of
    the way, and none in the way itself.

Bringing in what is to be brought
in its season —
harvest of all kinds.
So simple that it will not do
for those who do not understand simplicity.
The loose change
spills through relaxed hands.
(We are not as loose
as we think we are.
Complexion of the way.
It is hard not to ask
a hand up
        (out)
Yet and yet —
the spite holds close —
and we are the edge of it.
(Often the ghost
of the same thing
surprises
after the fact
of surprise.
The flag in the dark,
a light somewhere
against it.
Do not fear,
or let the fear be,
basis for the fact.

Presumption had it
from the start.
There was no certainty
except in thinking —
and the thinking
one man's arrogance,
supported by his fellows
-theirs-
and what they could add
as well as support.

    The Interlocutor:
    No reasons. We have run out of them. The ages tend
    to coalesce. In every part the story is the same. Nor is
    their outcome  legitimate issue.  It is borne on simply
    by another story.

The quick heat of the past —
the past known
                    only
in its heat,
and from the fan of certain flames.
Embers kicked at times,
enough to make another blaze.
but first, the smoke.
We do not burn the bones
in our firing,
with any wisdom,
let them go unevenly
in what decays.
Purpose of the past.
Well,
          there are those
who talk its uses,
and created substrata
into a remembrance
-black-
          a trace of form
along black coal.
An instruction, perhaps,
but not in forms
with other story —
simply what is,
and kicks among
dust and flour sand,
shifting always,
desert to desert.

        The Interlocutor:
        I would not like to be remembered solely as the one
        who stood at one side, recorded, and made some
        comment. Of all this work, and in it, I have had some
        hand, though not a great one. The highest moment
        would be one in which I recorded my own movements
        accurately.

Break, as a step,
and not a fracture.
The fracture is only a device
to get attention

to a hurt.
The time break is another thing,
and sets another face
in facet and prism
to the light of the sun.
Take leave in leisure,
the looser line of working —
no less serious.
An equation comes,
but it is not an easy one.
Nor will it,
in its own willing
come back to pattern
-if one *is* remembered.
Only the residue —
the cruelties —
the arrogance —
a few times the warmth.
We have named it 'human'
equalling compassion
with an ideal:
humanity.
Another arrogance.
It is as truly
the property of stones and stars
and water.
The center is a fortune
moved by current
along the sea.
It does not sleep there,
nor does it rise
from arrogance.
The pride in things
is pride of life.
It does not center
in a man,
nor in his works.
It will not parallel
in wind or life
to greed or violence.

    The Interlocutor:
    In the words themselves there may be something

In the words themselves there may be something useful which has nothing to do with their configurations, or patterns one with another. They have been made, yet they have grown their own ways — apart from the making.

Where there are records
they will only serve
until that place is reached
where fear of what was known
demands a falsehood,
for a power equally false,
that contrived fabric is in danger,
if the present is to survive.
(Because we cannot have more
than one present at a time,
we tend to hold on.)
And yet that way will lose
the very thing it tries to hold.
Accounts are due,
and debts will have their way —
their payment.
And on the beach,
where I have picked up glass,
the shard of yesterday,
it is no less than paving stones,
or spear points.
Graffiti and detritus
must remain the same,
no matter where we found them,
or in our time sense
which one was prior.
A long season must extend,
extenuate the case?
There is no thing anywhere
to warrant it.
The guilt is nothing moral
in our enclosure —
but there is guilt against ourselves,
and what we are
is everywhere the same.
Stones sweat a water

similar to blood.
There are the proofs:
Nothing given is proof
for other than itself.
The artifacts are covered and uncovered,
wind and sand and water
play among them,
knowing nothing of concern.
One pocket empties
into another pocket.
What more to say?

Perhaps the cruelty is shadow.
In a glass, it moves form.
Again, and then again.
Ideas around us are alive,
but not as ideas —
separate as we,
and joined as we.
Whatever tampers, does so
in a context
            willing it.
Emotion is the wind.
The sea.
            The salt is blood,
Eat hearty.
            Morning comes.

## CODETTA

Returned to the sea itself,
from rains that fall
along the interior hills,
a distillate, and leached
of properties that flow again,
and reach the water
-debouch in delta-
sexual figure —
the rivers to the sea.
The tribes converge again
-take up old ways
as surely as the prior flints
worn smooth,
but with the trace of edge
to be remembered and reworked.
Sails to rig,
and hulls to keel.
In same breath
to leave the powers to themselves —
the lands and seas
to work our follies
in the primal sense —
convergence working —
break down our histories —
now loam and compost.
Tide and wind —
their thrust in it.
The use is minimal
barring pillage.
(I rattle at the gates —
a human cage.)
The flex of muscle,
not the toughness of a scar.

Where is the back country?
Who is it lives there?
The remote is often forefront,
and foreshore behind.
Those countries ranging
from the pole star
to the tidelands —

under Orion and Cassiopeia.
Walking a night road, he said:

Kris Larson,
East Machias,
10/5/77

"For all I may have learned in knowing,
I have lost the sense of stars,
in their naming, and their figures."
A loss which many tend to leave
and walk away from.
The subliminal does come up again —
some of it exactly
-at the moment-
others entered in another place.
The flow both ways,
reverse of tide.
There is expression,
                    direct,
in all its indirection.

Replacement is concern,
not covered by nostalgia.
It will not be what it was,
and yet it is —
always that, and nothing more./
We redeem our movements.
We do not redeem the past.
It is no prize,
in longer lines
no forfeit.
What we in the mind's eye
contemplate
is all there is.
The mention becomes the fact.

They spoke of census,
after the land was settled,
but the settlers resented it —
that their affairs be known.
These were the quarrels
                    (and are)
set over from the first heroics.
No questions settled —
nor can questions die
in answers.
There are no ends

as opening —
to leave or stay —
it is an opening that stays
in everything.
All places come as equal.
What is of power,
what is the object
or the mover
                    stands
as equal.
There are no places,
nothing thought of —
nothing preconceived.
The muscle, flexing,
moves as little as the wish.
The laughter is its own —
the sorrow.
Ritual and ceremony
stand alone, inscrutable.
They have not evolved from us.
We have looked on,
and seen, as bystanders,
what we thought was controlled.
It was done and finished
before we appeared.
There is no loosening,
and nothing tightened.

In the first of it,
we speak of mornings,
and the freshness.
We tire easily, and see
our tiring.
                    Nothing.
The vision blurs.
That writing which continues
moves off the page.
Blood runs, not needs a vein.
There is a madness
in exactitude —
the rain or wind —
or both against a rock.
Tide - diurnal.

Somewhere and nowhere
make the place,
as place, perhaps itself
without the knowledge,
or feel of a direction.
The sea in rise
or fall —
　　　　　　a source
in what surrounds the sea.
The numbers continue,
and in their rising,
fall implicit.
It is that other
which we do not name,
and cannot sense
by anything we hold
as ours —
the black holes, settled
in among the seeming movement,
what will draw us in,
nor in any place give out again.
Another cycle,
parallel to life and death and love,
but where those turns
or any others
fall apart.
They cannot reach, and cannot touch.
For us, there is nothing
we may reach
　　　　　　　　beyond the context
where we are.
And taken rightly
it *is* the answer:
All in all.
That what we do conceive
is everywhere, and possible,
but that we do not
embrace the whole of it
within ourselves.
That was the first and primal arrogance.
To know was not to do,
nor to attempt.

The chain reaction holds,
the tampering destroys.
His story. Once.
For all times his.
We move beyond it,
placing it as ours.


**End Book Five of Ranger**

Truro, Massachusetts, July 15, 1971
Temple, Maine, October 15, 1977